Praise for *FLAUNT!*

"*FLAUNT!* is a reassuring reminder to us gals that we are not alone in this crazy journey to become fulfilled and self-actualized. If you are searching for insight, wisdom, logic, intuition, emotion, and humor, read this book. Get out your highlighting pen — you'll need it!"

— **Lannie Garrett,** singer/entertainer and
Colorado Music Hall of Fame inductee

"In order for each of us to fully express our gifts in the world, we must combine the masculine and feminine parts in ourselves — the drive, on the one hand, and what Lora Cheadle calls the 'sparkle,' on the other. Whatever you desire to create in your life, Lora's combination of practical insight and contagious enthusiasm will help you get there."

— **Kelly Notaras,** author of *The Book You Were Born to Write*

"*FLAUNT!* is a fabulously important book for all women! Too many wonderful women underestimate themselves and need more self-esteem. Lora Cheadle has hit it out of the ballpark with her glorious book!"

— **Stephanie Blake,** actor, two-time
Miss Exotic World Pageant winner, and burlesque legend

"Sage and refreshingly honest, Lora Cheadle's *FLAUNT!* provides a playful path for women to unapologetically integrate all of themselves to live and work with more passion, creativity, and freedom. Whether you've defined your self-worth by what you've achieved, you've squashed your own dreams in order to support someone else's, or you want to shed self-judgment and rewire your brand (and your body!) to choreograph a different kind of life for yourself, you're going to love this book!"

— **Alexia Vernon,** author of *Step into Your Moxie*

"Reveals tips on how burlesque will empower women's lives."
— **Leslie Zemeckis,** actress, author,
and award-winning documentarian

"Written like you're talking with your best, wisest, and funniest girlfriend, *FLAUNT!* is a must-read for all women (and men) who need new tools and a path forward to be their best and happiest selves."

— **Kathleen Nalty,** founder of the
Center for Legal Inclusiveness

FLAUNT!

DROP YOUR COVER & REVEAL YOUR SMART, SEXY & SPIRITUAL SELF

LORA CHEADLE

New World Library
Novato, California

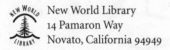 New World Library
14 Pamaron Way
Novato, California 94949

The material in this book is intended for education. No expressed or implied guarantee of the effects of the use of the recommendations can be given or liability taken. The author's experiences used as examples throughout this book are true, although identifying details such as names and locations have been changed to protect privacy.

Life Choreographer® and Life Choreography® are registered trademarks of Lora Cheadle. Naked Self-Worth™ is a pending trademark of Lora Cheadle.

Text design by Tona Pearce Myers

Library of Congress Cataloging-in-Publication data is available.

First printing, November 2019
ISBN 978-1-60868-621-6
Ebook ISBN 978-1-60868-622-3
Printed in Canada on 100% postconsumer-waste recycled paper

 New World Library is proud to be a Gold Certified Environmentally Responsible Publisher. Publisher certification awarded by Green Press Initiative.

10   9   8   7   6   5   4   3   2   1

*To all the women who have cried in the shower,
smiled when they wanted to scream,
and couldn't wait to get home and unhook their bra.*

Contents

INTRODUCTION

The Curtain Rises

I believe that women deserve to be seen.

And I believe that universally women *want* to be seen. For who they are. Not for what they do. Not for who they are *in relation to* others, or what they can give. But for themselves. For who they are inside, at their most raw, authentic, vulnerable, and naked core.

I believe that when women are not seen, they cannot be accepted for who they are. When women are not accepted for who they are, they cover their power, dim their light, hide their beauty, and reject uninhibited joy. They lose what I like to call their *sparkle*, which is everything inside that makes them uniquely, authentically, and spectacularly themselves. When we lose our sparkle, we lose touch with our hearts, we suppress our personal desires, and we fall out of love with our bodies. In short, we fall into a state of chronic self-judgment, and we stop enjoying life fully.

I can hear you saying, "Oh, come now, Lora! Everyone gets those self-deprecating voices in their heads once in a while! It's not like I'm a pathetic, sniveling, groveling creature lying in a puddle on the floor. I'm a successful, happy adult."

And I say, "Yes, you are right! To a point. It's deeper, and more insidious, than that."

If you are anything like me, it's not the moments of *Oh gawd, I am such a freaking fat and out-of-shape loser* that send me spiraling down; it's the fact that nobody notices the things I do each and every day of my life that are, objectively, pretty incredible. It's the fact that for many others, I do, in fact, keep everything together. Yet nobody really sees me. They see only what's not done.

As cartoonist Bob Thaves said about Fred Astaire, "Sure he was great, but don't forget that Ginger Rogers did everything *he* did…backwards and in high heels."

We are so used to dancing backwards and in high heels that we lose sight of the fact that what we do, day in and day out, is extraordinary. We have been fighting for our rights, for our status, for recognition, and for our voice for so long — and we are *so stunningly capable* of molding ourselves into our high-heeled, backward-stepping dance — that we forget it is our right to turn around, take off our dysfunctional (but admittedly supercute and sometimes-totally-worth-the-pain) shoes, and dance our own dance. Our way.

Sure, as the song says, we can *bring home the bacon, fry it up in a pan, and never let you forget you're a man,* but is that even what we want? I don't know about you, but as a little girl, I dreamed of being a sparkly fairy princess or a ballerina. I dreamed of things that made me happy. I didn't dream of mainlining coffee so I had enough energy to power through my days or of being more focused on completing my never-ending to-do list than on grounding into the joy of the present moment and actually enjoying my life. I didn't dream of sacrificing myself so that others could shine. Or of constantly molding myself into some unattainable idea of perfection.

So I ask you, what happened to pursuing *our* dreams and desires?

It's my guess that, like me, you have lived your life covering your body, your brains, and your beliefs, somewhat terrified that someone, somewhere, might (*gasp!*) get the "wrong idea" about you. It's time to reveal yourself. To find what I like to call your Naked Self-Worth™, which is the ability to value yourself for who you are instead of what others believe you should be, without seeking to please or conform, and to stand unapologetically in your raw truth, knowing that who you are is more than enough. Through the five steps of *FLAUNT!* you will develop your Naked Self-Worth, expose the authentic woman you are underneath, and find your sparkle, so you can waltz into a deeply satisfying life that is happy, healthy, and burnout-free.

Whether it's self-judgment, body shame, fear, an insatiable need for approval, or some other experience or story that you've internalized, *FLAUNT!* uses burlesque as the vehicle to strip away the costumes and masks you have been wearing, release unreasonable expectations, and put down everything that's holding you back from loving yourself and your life fully.

Through the five steps of *FLAUNT!* I will share the story of how I went from overachieving lawyer to fully embodied burlesque star and female-empowerment coach, empowering you to reconnect with *your* inner burlesque star — to strip out of body shame, guilt, self-judgment, and whatever stories and beliefs are holding you back — so you, too, can *FLAUNT!* your smart, sexy, and spiritual self, exactly as you are, in a way that is perfect for you!

Ummm, Why Burlesque?

Now, if you are reading this and thinking, *No way! I could never show off my sagging breasts, C-section scar, cellulite, muffin top* (or whatever body part you are hating on at the moment)… what I want to say to you is this: *FLAUNT!* is not about getting naked physically!

Unless, of course, you want to.

FLAUNT! is about using the principles of burlesque to strip away everything nonessential that's covering your raw, beautiful soul, to strip down emotionally, intellectually, and maybe even physically, so you can reveal your whole self to the world exactly as you are, with divine, uninhibited authenticity and acceptance.

The other thing I want to say is: *Even if it were* about getting physically naked, you are more than your breasts, or even your picture-perfect thigh gap. You are more than your insecurities, your fears, or your failures. You are more than a successfully completed to-do list or a cushy paycheck. Developing compassion for the parts that you do not love unlocks a deep feminine wisdom that reminds you that the very thing scaring you is the key that opens the door to your sense of unshakable worthiness. It is from this space that healing begins, and you can reclaim and fall in love with yourself, your body, and your life. And if you don't believe me right now, that's okay, too. Creating, and embodying, your burlesque identity will help you get there!

Let me explain what I mean by getting naked and being seen. When was the last time you looked at yourself in the mirror and *saw* the truth of the woman staring back at you? When was the last time you let another see her? I know how scary it is to be honest and vulnerable about yourself, but I also know that our fears are oftentimes much greater than the actual thing we're afraid of, and until we move into those fears, we are held captive by them.

Not only does being brave enough to *FLAUNT!* your beauty, your brains, and your beliefs change you for good, but it changes our world. And living with your smart, sexy, spiritual self fully exposed allows you to be seen for the glittery burlesque goddess or the badass bitch you are. When we reclaim our power, diversity, and voice, one woman at a time, we create change.

If you're feeling kind of scared by this whole *naked* thing, I'm right there with you! I know how you feel, because once upon a time, I was scared, too. I was scared that I wasn't enough. That I wasn't pretty enough, or smart enough, or strong enough. That I would not be accepted for who I really was. My biggest fear was that I'd put it all out there, I'd show my raw self, and I'd be dismissed as unworthy. I'd find out that I had been right all along: that I *wasn't* enough. And I'd be left standing there. Exposed. With nowhere to hide and with nothing to cover myself.

After ten years of practicing law and after a lifetime of being a really good girl, I'd personally had enough. Enough of the cover-up. Enough of always trying to do more. So, I decided to get naked and reveal myself — literally. In my midforties, I became a burlesque dancer, and it set me free! Being brave enough to get naked meant that there was nothing left for me to hide and, consequently, nothing left to fear. Cellulite, stretch marks, my exhaustion…my fear that no one would see me — or value me, or love me — unless I conformed to their standards…I put it all out there, without cover. I allowed others to see me as I was. *I was seen.* And I learned that who I am is more than enough.

Think about it like this: In order for a gem to sparkle most brilliantly, all its facets must be exposed. If we want to sparkle as brilliantly as we are capable of sparkling, we must expose all facets of who we are as well.

Your sparkle is your sense of worth. The knowingness that who you are inside is perfect for you. What's covering your sparkle? Is it external factors, such as sexism, ageism, and racism? Or internal factors, such as body shame, mommy guilt, or the ideas, stories, and beliefs you hold that may no longer be true? When you get naked, and unapologetically expose all facets of who you are in everything that you do, you can't help but sparkle and shine!

Are you ready to be seen for who you are, as opposed to what you do or the clothing you wear? Are you ready to find congruence between your inner being, the roles you play, and the persona you present to the world? Are you ready to connect deeply with yourself and start living and enjoying the life you've worked so hard to create? Are you ready to stop putting yourself last and to experience uninhibited joy and fulfillment every day of your life, not just on occasion?

Yes? Then you are ready to *FLAUNT!*

Choreographing Your Life, and What You'll Find in This Book to Help You

Since the three-act structure of beginning, middle, and end is used universally in storytelling and dance choreography, so too does *FLAUNT!* follow this structure to sashay you through the three acts of your own life: past, present, and future.

Act I, "Recognize & Release," is your past. Your heritage, culture, and entire history, including all the key experiences or stories in your life that have made you the woman you are today. Act I is where you take an honest look at your labels, roles, scripts, and masks; the costumes you wear; and the overarching theme of your life; and ask, "Who has been choreographing my life for me, what exactly have they created, and is my life, the way it stands now, even something I want?" Recognition makes you aware of what is, or is not, serving you and what inhibitions you may need to release in order to soar and be seen and accepted for all that you truly are.

In Act II you "Reveal" who you are, exclusive of everything that you recognized and released in Act I. This is where you boldly meet and claim your inner burlesque star, and where you learn to return an answer to the trite cocktail-hour question "So, what do you do?" that goes much deeper than merely stating your job title and relationship status. In Act II you will be introduced to the five steps of *FLAUNT!* and will dance your way through the first three so you can reclaim your joy and bravely incorporate your authentic self back into your life. Here's a sneak peek at the five steps:

F̱LAUNT! Step 1: F̱ind Your Fetish
FḺAUNT! Step 2: Ḻaugh Out Loud
FLA̱U̱NT! Step 3: A̱ccept U̱nconditionally
FLAUṈT! Step 4: Ṉavigate the Negative
FLAUNṮ! Step 5: Ṯrust Your Truth

Act III, "Re-choreograph," moves you through the final two steps of *FLAUNT!* and provides tips, tools, and tricks for re-choreographing a future that allows you to meet your responsibilities but still dance the dance you were born to perform. Free from self-judgment and self-sacrifice, from a life lived from the neck up, disconnected from your body, your spirit, and your own core essence. Here you learn how to embrace your own imperfect womanhood, free from inhibition and with the ability to be the joyous, satisfied — dare I say — *sparkly* being you were meant to be!

What Is Burlesque?

No, I'm *not* talking about a movie with Cher and Christine Aguilera. Burlesque is a glittery, glamorous, and oftentimes humorous extravaganza that originated in Europe over 150 years ago. It continued in America through the vaudeville circuits; into the glamorous forties, fifties, and sixties; all the way to the present day through the neo-burlesque resurgence. Although some people think that burlesque is stripping, it isn't. Burlesque is a theatrical experience where the audience purchases a ticket to the show; they do not pay or tip dancers to take off more clothes or to give them personalized attention. The point of a burlesque show is to provoke thought, laughter, and teasing entertainment. It is not about inspiring lust. In fact, although many burlesque performers go down to pasties (nipple covers, often with tassels) and panties, full nudity is not allowed.

Burlesque is a parody, a grand and dazzling spectacular that points out the various juxtapositions or ironies present in everyday life and mocks many of society's uptight views. Using humor, exaggeration, and daring, burlesque showcases that which is right in front of our eyes but we choose not to see. Which is what makes the removal of clothing so powerful: nudity is taboo! Burlesque pokes fun at the fact that sex, age, sexuality, and non-Photoshopped bodies are all things that we have but deny about ourselves to others.

Performers tease the audience by making them think they are going to see something they shouldn't see and then pulling it away. A good performer creates anticipation by concealing and revealing that which lies beneath her elaborate costume, always leaving the audience wanting more. Like so many other things in life, burlesque is all about the tease! When our desires and rewards are dangled just outside our reach, it entices us, keeps us playing the game, hanging on, and wanting more!

In burlesque lingo, whenever an article of clothing is removed, it's called a *reveal*. Each reveal provides the audience with a little bit more information, shows them a bit more, and gives them enough satisfaction to keep them watching, always waiting for more. Burlesque is interactive. The emcee in a burlesque show typically begins by explaining to the audience that burlesque is not like traditional theater. If you see something you like and want to see more, holler! Whistle! Have fun and show your appreciation! Let the dancers know that you acknowledge their bravery. Their daring. Let them know that they are being seen and accepted. Sometimes, when an audience is too quiet, burlesque performers even put their hand to their ear, like, *Are you there? I can't hear you!*

The idea of burlesque is to show who we are, without our masks, without our carefully constructed facades. In burlesque, as in *FLAUNT!*, the removal of clothing signals the removal of a cultural norm, an ironic idea, a label, a role, or even a belief. For example, as polite members of society, none of us are supposed to admit that we are curious about seeing others naked. But come on! We all are! Everyone sneaks peeks — and no, not in a sexual way! As women, we check out other women. We compare our bodies, our hair, our makeup, or *whatever* to those of other women. This sense of curiosity is what creates anticipation in a burlesque routine. *Are we going to see something we aren't supposed to see? And how will I compare?* Burlesque is not about the strip; it's about the tease!

The Spiritual Tease

It's odd to say, but my own spiritual self-growth journey mirrored the concepts found in burlesque: tease, voyeurism, and slow reveal. As a constant seeker of truth, I'd reach a new level of understanding, only to realize there was yet another layer to unveil. Which flummoxed me completely at times! I'd watch others, do what they did, meditate, read, and take classes. I'd study the great masters from around the world, do exactly what they did, but then I'd have a bad-hair day on the same day as a catastrophic hard-drive failure while uploading pictures of my son for his middle-school-graduation slide show (at the eleventh hour), and I'd come totally unhinged. It was almost like peace was a thing that the Universe would dangle in front of me, tease me mercilessly with, but never quite let me have. *Just read one more book, Lora! If you would have only meditated this morning, you would have been fine, Lora! But how sad for you; you didn't quite make it! Better luck next time!*

How ironic that actual burlesque facilitated my process of self-discovery on a spiritual level. Just like burlesque performers let go of their clothing, I let go of my own limiting judgments and beliefs. I shed society's labels, my own limited interpretation of myself and my roles, slowly at first and then with increasing fervor and joy. Stripped bare, the truth of my heart and soul visible for all to see, my own sparkle was exposed. I no longer had to guess who I was or what I wanted. I knew. And with that knowledge, I could re-choreograph my life as it was meant to be. Sparkly, brilliant, and more magnificently fun than I had ever dreamed!

And just like in burlesque shows, where the audience cheers wildly with the removal of each article of clothing, encouraging the performer to *reveal more*, so too did my friends and family cheer me wildly on as I removed layer upon layer of limiting judgments and beliefs. Through my journey I had unknowingly given others permission to begin their own burlesque, to reveal themselves, and to finally, gratefully, have the opportunity to be seen and accepted for who they were.

My foray into the world of burlesque showed me that burlesque is a joyful experience for the performers and audience alike because it busts stereotypes and celebrates women of all shapes, sizes, abilities, and ages. Burlesque is not about looking a certain way; it is about reveling in one's reality. While other middle-aged moms flocked to me, larger women flocked to the larger burlesque performers, and flat-chested women crushed on the flat-chested performers. Seeing performers who looked like them, with what they *perceived* to be their same flaws, but who dared to be confident, beautiful, sexy, or funny in spite of those flaws, set them free to embrace those same qualities in themselves.

The act of watching someone *just like* them shed the label of *fat*, *flat-chested*, *old*, or *ugly* and be seen in all their glittery, flawed gloriousness was enough for some women to loosen their own labels. Watching their favorite performer do all they wished *they* could do, seeing others react encouragingly to their visibility, empowered many women to believe that they could let go and show their true selves as well. With its focus on humor and female-dominated power, burlesque gives women explicit permission to live confidently, joyfully, and without cover.

Is it any wonder that throughout my metamorphosis into an actual burlesque dancer I had so many friends watching my every move? Every layer of fear or expectation that I broke through — every label, role, or script that I challenged, reinterpreted, or removed — gave them permission to do the same. If I could be outrageously happy in spite of my imperfections, so could they. As I broke what I perceived to be "the rules," I proved to myself that there was nothing stopping me from building my dreams and living my sparkle, except me.

The laughter, parody, and joy in the face of taboo and

judgment that burlesque provided were the ideal combination to heal wounds around body image, sexuality, self-judgment, gender roles, power, shame, or guilt. Without setting foot on an actual stage, many of my friends were able to strip out of the fear, lies, and inhibitions that had been placed on them by their culture, family, or religion — or that were self-imposed. Just as my childhood belief that I needed to be perfect in order to be worthy became my metaphoric *corset of perfection*, so too could others find ways to release their own inhibitions.

Not only had I disrobed physically but I was disrobing emotionally, too, by living my particular brand of sparkle. Society said that a middle-aged mom, lawyer, and spirit-based female-empowerment coach shouldn't do what I was doing. But I did it anyway. Not to rebel or to create a fuss, but because it was in *my* heart to do it. I was no longer worried about *looking like* I was doing the right things for the right reasons or being what I thought others wanted me to be. I was interested in getting metaphorically naked and revealing everything there was about myself.

And as a result, I was happier and more content than I had ever been. Accepting myself and my desires as they were freed me to dance my own dance with wild abandon, and that was exactly what I did!

Your Inner Burlesque Star

Your inner burlesque star is your naked, authentic self. She is the confident, fun, playful, anything-is-possible part of you who cannot be hurt by others, because she knows that accepting herself is the only thing that truly matters. Although she loves costumes, masks, makeup, feathers, glitter — the whole nine yards — she knows how to take it all off. She's not afraid to strip down, to show off her beauty, her brains, and her beliefs, exactly as they are. Without apology. Do you think you might want to hang out with her? She's pretty awesome!

Like playing an elaborate game of dress-up, *FLAUNT!* allows you to put on and take off a variety of personas. And just like in a real burlesque routine, strip out of the ones you find confining, outdated, or not to your liking. *FLAUNT!* is pure creative fun that does not require you to add to your already overly busy life. To the contrary, finding your inner burlesque star creates more space, grace, and joy in both your professional and your personal life because, like cleaning out your closet, clearing the clutter makes it easier to see and appreciate the goodness that remains.

Plus, it's fun! Creating a visual representation of your fears, insecurities, and judgments keeps it lighthearted and makes it easier to choose what to shed and what to keep. Burlesquing your life challenges you to remove your layers of judgment and protection, to face your fear of being naked — whether that nakedness is emotional, intellectual, or physical — by saucily stripping away the coverings you are most afraid to lose and offering up your raw, authentic self, without apology. And to do it all with a wink and a smile!

Are you ready for a burlesque dance party? Let's *FLAUNT!*

ACT I

RECOGNIZE & RELEASE

All the world's a stage,
And all the men and women merely players;
They have their exits and their entrances,
And one man [*ahem,* **woman**] in his [**her!**]
time plays many parts.

— WILLIAM SHAKESPEARE, *As You Like It*

*I*f, as Shakespeare so aptly pointed out, all the world's a stage and each of us are merely players, playing our parts until we fade away into oblivion, the question inevitably becomes "Who *is* choreographing your life?"

A choreographer is the person who composes the sequence of events or moves in a dance or a play, leading to a meaningful, cohesive, and purposeful performance. While it is sometimes appropriate to allow others to choreograph your life, it is all too easy to forget that the primary choreographer is *you*.

The Legacy of Regret

Let me tell you a story. I was close to both my grandmothers, who, by the standards of their day, were pretty perfect women. Although I assumed there were things about them that I didn't have the full scoop on, I felt like I really knew them. But after they passed away, I learned I had been wrong. I found out that these women were so much more than they shared with me, our family, or the rest of the world. And because they had kept parts of themselves hidden, their true essence had been lost forever, not only to themselves but to all of us who loved them.

I am not making this up. On her deathbed, my grandma looked up at my dad (who is hugely into genealogy) and said,

"You know those stories about my father, and how mean he could be? Don't ever worry that anger is in your lineage, because I was adopted."

And then she died.

We never had the chance to learn anything more or to ask questions. We knew her, but we didn't know her at all. Because she was afraid that others would not accept her if they *found out*, she had covered up a key piece of herself and our family's history. Although we were grateful she finally revealed herself to us and allowed us to integrate this tidbit of information, it was kind of too late, because we never had the opportunity to see her naked and exposed, for exactly who she was!

And then there was my maternal grandma. While refraining from any deathbed bombshells, she left us with just as many questions as grandma number one. Of course I knew she was smart. She had jumped ahead two years in school and had attended a private university during World War II, dropping out to get married after my grandfather came home. Sometimes she would write poems and stories that were so good that I'd ask whose they were because I was certain they were copied from some famous work, but they were always hers. Which was cool, but I never really gave it a second thought.

That is, until she died. Sure, I had seen her scrapbooks and heard her funny story about sunbathing in a cemetery with her sorority sisters and getting caught by the nuns, but her scrapbooks and stories were just the tip of the vast iceberg of who she was as a person and as a woman. Although before her death she had been honest in sharing her dissatisfaction with her own life, we couldn't understand or appreciate the depth of that pain because we had never been allowed to see fully who she was.

After she passed away, we found journals and notebooks, where she drew incredible pictures, wrote breathtaking poems, and related stories that provided rich insight into her, her marriage, and the world. Not just into her as a wife, mom, or school secretary but as a woman, and the pain she experienced in covering her sparkle and light and being everything she thought she was supposed to be instead. She kept much of her intellect and passions hidden, and as a result, her life was never that happy or that fulfilled.

Wearing masks, covering themselves with the requisite costumes of the day, and dancing choreography that was not their own robbed these two women of themselves and their capacity to experience authentic joy and fulfillment. But it also robbed us of the ability to know, or see, or grow through them and the stories of their lives.

I don't know about you, but when I die, I don't want my family going through my things and feeling that sense of loss, that sense of *If I had only known*...about me. I want to express myself fully, to be seen and known, for everything that I am deep inside, giving myself the opportunity to live fully, joyously, and intimately connected to those I love. Now. Not after I die.

I can only imagine the legacy my two grandmas could have left, had they been brave enough to reveal themselves fully. To show who they were. To allow themselves to be expansive, seen, and accepted as they truly were. What about you? What is your legacy?

When was the last time you were giddy with anticipation over something you were about to do? When you knew that what you wanted to do made little or no practical sense, but you knew you had to try or you'd regret it forever? No matter how old you are, no matter what you look like or sound like, it's never too late. In fact, the older you are, the more imperative it is to begin now! So, if there is anything in you that wants something more, you owe it to yourself to give it a try, to create your legacy…or you risk regretting it forever.

For me, it was dance. What could it be for you?

CHAPTER I

The Labels, Roles & Scripts of My Emerging Womanhood

*L*et me share with you the labels, roles, and scripts of my past. The accompanying costumes, accessories, and dance steps that were all a part of the choreography created for me by others. Why? Because oftentimes we see aspects of ourselves in the stories of others, bringing us levels of insight that we didn't have before. What I want for you is to be able to recognize and release the choreography that no longer serves you so you can dance your dance, your own way. To see how my past informed my present, how it almost dictated my future, and how I used *FLAUNT!* to set myself free from constantly seeking external validation and find joy and satisfaction beyond what I thought possible.

What I wanted, deep in my soul, was to be wickedly smart, without being labeled an aggressive bitch. To be powerfully spiritual, using and developing my own intuition on my own terms, without being called a New Age, woo-woo freak. To be sexy as hell, my own way, and enjoy how my body looked and felt, without being called a slut. I wanted to flaunt and to *be* all that I *was* without apology and most certainly without cover. Without checking pieces of me at the door when I went into a professional environment, and without altering or limiting myself to suit others. I wanted to flaunt myself, not to be obnoxious but to allow myself the opportunity to live the full breadth of all that I was. Part Amazon warrior, part gangly pink flamingo, part regal countess, part traditional June Cleaver, part ethereal goddess. I wanted to set all of me free, to show myself and the world everything I was capable of. Without worrying *what people might think.*

What Women Should Do, Think, Believe, and Wear

I was a successful corporate attorney with a good life. I had a husband, two children, and a house, and everything was fine. *Normal.* Just what it was supposed to be. It was just that most days felt like a sprint to a finish line that was constantly being moved one mile farther away. No matter how hard I tried, I could never please everyone, get it all done, or look the way I wanted to look. Collapsing into bed, sometimes in the same yoga pants I had collapsed into bed in the night before, I'd wonder, *Is this really all there is? Because, seriously, there's got to be something more!*

I think we've probably all had times when we've been overwhelmed and frustrated without really knowing why or having any idea what to do about it. My solution was to randomly invest in self-help books, sign up for personal-development seminars, schedule in more regular spa days, and rope my family into morning meditation. *There, that should do it!* If I were somehow on the proverbial "wrong path," I sure as heck was going to figure it out and get myself, my life, and my family back on track. Perhaps you may have gone down this road a time or two? I thought so.

With my family rolling their eyes and finding excuses to skip out of family meditation hour, I homed in on *finding my life purpose* and *living my highest good*, making these concepts the gold standards to which I aspired. I was certain that finding these magical yet elusive things would put me on the "right path" (even if my wayward family chose not to come along) and give me the joyful, meaningful, and chaos-free life filled with intimacy and connection that I craved.

But try as I might, I couldn't figure out how to put *living my highest good* or *finding my life purpose* on my vision board, because I had no idea what those concepts really meant — they just sounded good. Like things I "should" aspire to, because if I somehow achieved them, my frustration would magically go away. And, as I'm sure you can guess, nothing ever really changed.

Which, ironically, was kind of a relief. Because the idea of disrupting my carefully orchestrated life was scary, too! Building my so-called perfect life had been no small task, and I wasn't about to let it go in search of some elusive New Age concept. You see, my life wasn't really about me anymore. I had a family who needed me to care for them; that's what mattered now. Never mind that I had never moved to New York or Los Angeles, auditioned for the Rockettes, or trekked through Europe. I was *his wife, their mom,* and Lora Cheadle, *Esquire,* now. And proper wives, moms, and lawyers weren't sexy. Or flirty. Or daring. Or too smart. Or too powerful.

So I stayed safely in my role of corporate wife, suburban mom, and competent woman, dancing within the bounds of the neat little box — labeled "what your life should look like" — in which I lived, performing the same worn-out choreography that I had been given, while feeling slightly dissatisfied and disconnected. From my life, but more importantly, from me.

Finding My *FLAUNT!*

With an explosion of color, *FLAUNT!* woke me up to the fact that I had spent my life dancing choreography that was not my own. I had let others choose the music, the costumes, and even the stage on which I was supposed to perform. I had willingly cloaked myself with costumes, labels, roles, and scripts that were not mine. In my quest for "perfect womanhood" I had inadvertently hidden my true self and dulled my own sparkle. *FLAUNT!* made me realize that in order to be happy and healthy and to joyfully dance my own life, I didn't need to do more or try harder.

What I needed was to strip out of all that I had layered on in an attempt to be what I was "supposed to be" and expose myself exactly as I was. *FLAUNT!* showed me that I was a smart, capable, and dedicated mom, wife, and career woman, who also happened to be smart, sexy, and spiritual. *And that was okay!* Revealing my truth, my core essence, the divine goddess I was inside, and bringing in all versions of everything I had ever been, empowered me to re-choreograph a new life that was more spectacular, more satisfying, and more fully my own than I had ever dreamed possible.

Through the five steps of *FLAUNT!* — Find Your Fetish, Laugh Out Loud, Accept Unconditionally, Navigate the Negative, and Trust Your Truth — and using burlesque as the vehicle, you can recognize and release the inhibitions and judgments that are covering you; reveal all facets of your authentic, core self (*ahem*, your inner burlesque star); and re-choreograph a brilliant, connected, and deeply satisfying life that reveals your beauty, brains, and beliefs so you can find the authentic joy, fulfillment, and self-acceptance that you crave. Are you ready to find your Naked Self-Worth and to sparkle? Then let's *FLAUNT!*

The Costumes and Steps Required
for the Dance of Perfect Womanhood

Most of us have been wearing the costumes of the roles we play for so long that we're not even aware that we are wearing them. We play a million different roles and have a million different responsibilities, and knowing our roles so well, we are adept at quick costume changes, of switching seamlessly between our various identities. Yet while we are often clear on how to live up to these roles, we are rarely clear on how to live up to being ourselves.

Growing up, I asked myself what I wanted to do with my life, not who I wanted to be. I never asked myself, *Who are you, Lora, deep inside, exclusive of your labels, roles, and scripts, and what kind of a woman would you like to be?* or *What do you need to do in order to create and sustain internal satisfaction, despite external circumstances?* No, I was more focused on answering questions like, *Where should I go to college? What should I major in to ensure that I get a job?* and *What are the next steps to take in order to achieve my career goals?* Nor did I ever sit down and plan out how I was going to do what I aspired to do while still being who I authentically was. You may have been the same way, more focused on doing than being. And it's my hunch that you never asked yourself deep, provocative questions about who you were inside and how you were going to integrate your honest expression of self with all that you wanted to do, either.

In my case, I modeled the behavior of those I loved, adopted the actions of those I admired, emulated beliefs of those I respected, and fumbled my way into adulthood, for right or for wrong. I'm guessing that I'm not alone, and like mine, many of your identities were created inadvertently over time, with little or no conscious awareness on your part of how they showcased or masked the woman you were inside.

Come with me, as I reveal the stories that created me, the masks that hid me, the costumes that enhanced me, and the roles in which I was cast.

My Childhood: The Tightly Corseted Little Princess

If you have seen a sitcom or a movie about a stereotypical family from the late seventies or early eighties, then you know much about my life. I had an unremarkably *normal*, white, Protestant, middle-class childhood, smack-dab in the middle of the good old US of A. Probably the only feature that made my family distinctive was that I was an only child, an only grandchild on both sides, and the only great-grandchild.

Yes, I was spoiled, but as the pride and joy of so many adults, I had to be perfect, because I was the only one. In order to get the praise that I so desperately desired, I had to live up to everyone's expectations, and I laced those expectations, like a corset, around the foundation of my being, dancing everybody else's choreography and making myself into exactly what others wanted me to be.

But, as perfect as I tried to be, I was still a free-spirited, fun-loving little girl, and there was no better way to express myself than through dance. Dancing got me out of my head and enabled me to flow free. Not only did dance provide an outlet for everything that was inside me; it also necessitated fancy dresses, sequins, rhinestones, tiaras, and feathers. I loved makeup, glitter, fancy hairstyles, and everything beautiful, feminine, and larger than life — exactly what my tightly laced soul wanted me to be!

This is how my journey into "perfect womanhood" began, and how my foundation was created. No matter what roles I added to my repertoire, and no matter what costumes I wore, underneath I kept the role of the perfect little princess alive and well, corseting myself into the ideals others set forth for me and oftentimes putting my own needs last. Much of my sense of worth came from how well I could please others, doing what they expected, following their rules, and dancing the dance they choreographed for me. Never mind that I sometimes had to cover, or mask, my true self in order to comply.

My Adolescence: Girls Who Wear Glasses

As a preteen, although ready to take off the tightly laced corset of my childhood and begin creating some of my own choreography, I was way too self-conscious and softhearted to show my peers who I really was and risk rejection. After all, I was not a jock or one of the pretty, popular girls. I was a studious ballet dancer who loved horses.

To make matters worse, I had recently gotten glasses — huge, round things with swooping sides and a hint of lavender — and popular girls didn't wear glasses! Since being a nerd was not what I aspired to, I wore my smart-girl glasses only in class, when I wanted to see the chalkboard, shoving them in my purse between classes and squinting my way down the hall the rest of the time. Because my parents said embarrassing and unhelpful things like "Just be yourself, sweetie!" I looked to my peers for interpretation of what made preteen girls fabulous, popular, and worthy. And because the image I saw looked nothing like me, I knew that covering up was my only option.

I surmised that if I could make myself look like a popular girl on the outside, nobody would notice that I was a total misfit on the inside. Great plan, right? Covering my body with the requisite dress code meant Levi's 501 jeans and IZOD polos, with a coordinating ribbon around the neck and Nike tennis shoes. Except that my family didn't have room for extras in the budget, and name-brand clothes were definitely extras. Not to be deterred, I focused my back-to-school shopping efforts on obtaining suitable knockoffs. JCPenney had polos with a fox instead of an alligator that I could obscure with the ribbon, leaving me confident that others would think it was an alligator, but the coveted Nikes were too expensive. Kinney Shoes had knockoff tennis shoes with a whale-shaped logo instead of the real Nike swoosh, and better yet, the knockoff pair came in lavender!

Happily covered in my knockoff popular-girl clothing, I marched to school, where the most popular, gorgeous eighth-grade boy *ever* looked down at my bright white shoes with the lavender whale swoosh, smirked, and said, "What kind of shoes are *those*?"

If you were ever an insecure adolescent girl, then you may relate to my level of mortification. I might as well have been naked, I felt so exposed! Shoes that I dearly loved the night before now filled me with embarrassment. How could I have been so stupid as to pick lavender? Real Nikes weren't lavender! Those shoes had been a terrible cover.

Speaking of terrible covers, I was terribly weary of covering my love of school, reading, and studying. Although I had always excelled in school, my role of the good girl kept me quiet about my achievements. After all, good girls didn't brag or make others feel bad! If I couldn't express myself the way I wanted in the fashion arena, maybe I could drop my cover in the academic arena, play the role of smart girl, and stand proud in my lavender smart-girl glasses instead of hiding behind them.

I registered for a science class rumored to be taught by the hardest teacher at school. The first day of class, the teacher's antics did not disappoint. Pacing around the room, he gestured to the pull-down periodic table of the elements and carried on about how we needed to memorize that table by the end of the week. No problem, I was great at memorization!

The day of the test I was ready. Both to ace the test and to publicly step into my role as a smart girl. Handing out the test, our teacher once again launched into a lecture about not underestimating the difficulty of his class. *Get over it!* I answered back in my own mind. *Just give me the test; I've totally got this!* He glanced down, just as I rolled my eyes in emphasis to my thoughts.

His explosion was cataclysmic. There I sat, tears welling up behind my lavender smart-girl glasses with the swooping arms, all eyes trained on me, as he carried on about my wanton disrespect. He slapped the test down on my desk and announced that he would grade my quiz aloud, in front of the entire class.

Quivering, I pushed through the test. Thank God I knew all the answers! My intelligence would shine through, I would be seen and accepted as the "smart girl," and everything would be all right.

Whisking my paper off the desk, he graded aloud: "Class, let's see what Miss Plank thinks *Fe* stands for." And then shaking his head sorrowfully and rolling his eyes in mock disappointment, he'd look at my answer, one element at a time, and ask, "Class? What does Fe *really* stand for?" as if all my answers, which were correct, were wrong!

What had just happened? Showing my intelligence had gotten me nowhere and had actually embarrassed me further. Burning with emotion, I saw that there were other, hidden factors at play. And although I didn't understand those factors, I knew that if I wanted to succeed, I was going to have to cover my body, my brains, and my beliefs.

The Flirt in the Pom-Pom Skirt

By the time high school rolled around, MTV had taken the world by storm. On the days I was not wearing my pom-pom uniform, I wore cut-up sweatshirts, short skirts, fishnets, anklets, and high heels, just like the girls in the ZZ Top videos. As you can probably guess, revealing myself got me seen! But not in the way I anticipated.

To me, a lifelong dancer who was used to costumes and showing my body in leotards and tights, short skirts and revealing clothing meant nothing. I thought dressing in a way that was authentic to my dancer personality would show people who I really was: a dancer who loved school and was tired of corseting herself into perfect-princess-hood or hiding behind her smart-girl glasses and was ready to reveal herself authentically so she could be seen and accepted for all that she was. Apparently I was wrong.

The attention I received from wearing short skirts and heels to school, while intoxicating in some regards, was confusing. How could a simple skirt create such a stir, and why weren't the boys — in their tight corduroy Ocean Pacific shorts, which were much shorter than my skirts, and fitted tank tops — ogled in the same way I was? Seriously, what was the big deal about my clothing, and why did my level of undress matter more than who I was inside, what kind of person I was, or what I achieved academically? How was it that I could spend my whole life being a compliant, good little girl and barely get noticed, but show my body and — *bam!* — everybody noticed in a way that overshadowed everything else I had accomplished?

I didn't understand why I was called a slut for exposing too much of my body, when I wasn't doing anything that actually was slutty. And paradoxically, why I was called a prude and teased for being a "goody-goody" and looking like a librarian when I covered my body and hung out in the library. No matter which side of my personality I revealed, I couldn't win!

The turning point happened one spring day in choir when I bent down to grab my music folder from the bottom shelf of the music rack at the front of the room. The choir director, frustrated by the lively and unfocused mood of the class, seized the moment and claimed that the chaotic mood of the class was my fault, that I had *distracted* the boys with my outfit.

While my initial reaction was confusion and embarrassment at getting in trouble, the whistling and catcalls of my friends soon had me doubled over with laughter and filled with an unquenchable sense of power and glee. For the next fifty minutes, student after student dropped their pencil or accidentally spilled their music folder, asking me loudly if I could *please* pick it up for them. I rose stunningly to the occasion with as much exaggerated bending over and hair flipping as I could muster.

Being teenagers, we inferred that if bending over in a miniskirt and heels garnered that much of a reaction, the response provoked by a bathing suit would be epic! The next day I came to school in a bikini covered by a long, belted jacket. In the middle of class, one of the boys announced loudly, "Wow! It's getting hot in here!" at which point I stood up, said, "It sure is!" and took off my jacket.

My subsequent visit to the principal's office taught me that my body, and the way I revealed it, held an enormous amount of power. It also taught me that being smart and being sexy were mutually exclusive concepts, that women who tried to embody both would be judged harshly, and that any previous accomplishments would be immediately dismissed. I learned that most people didn't care what I did or did not do in actuality; they saw only my outfits, and not the person inside those outfits. It made no sense why I couldn't be both a good girl and a flirt who loved to show off.

Irritated by the narrow range of acceptable behavior for a smart, good girl and by the burgeoning rumors about my lack of virtue, I decided to rebel. I was tired of covering my intellect, my dorky passions, and my love of dance-inspired clothing. I had lived much of my life according to other people's standards, constantly seeking praise, and I was done trying to figure it all out and covering certain pieces of my identity.

My mission became to reveal it all! Well, not exactly to reveal my authentic self, because that would mean risking real rejection — I couldn't take that — but to reveal a bold, sexy, funny, in-your-face version of myself who could never be stung by rejection or rumors or by being misunderstood again. I disconnected from my body and covered the pain of not being seen or accepted for who I was with the wildest, sexiest outfits possible, doing and saying what others only dared to think. Inside I was still a good girl in glasses who wanted to please and be praised. Nothing had changed at all except my clothing, yet changing my clothing changed everything about the way I was perceived. And despite my cavalier, "nobody can hurt me" attitude, the gossip hurt deeply.

My body was not my heart, my soul, or my thoughts. How I showed or covered it had nothing to do with who I was, and I strove to be immune from comments about my virtue or lack of self-worth because of the way I showed off my body. I saw how the roles I played, the costumes I wore, and the labels others assigned to me became more real than who I actually was. If my coverings mattered more than who I was or what I accomplished, then why bother trying?

Embracing the Neutrals

Frustrated by not being seen for who I was inside or for all that I had rightfully accomplished, and confused by the backlash from revealing my body — and tired of working so hard, only to be overshadowed by rumors and falsehoods — I hoped that college could give me a fresh start. I wanted to meet new people who could finally see the real me. Not my corset of perfection from elementary school, not my smart-girl glasses or my denim miniskirt and heels, but *me*, and everything I was inside.

The only way I could think of to accomplish this was to let go of every costume, mask, role, or identity I had ever embodied. I strove to become neutral, transparent, flat, and free of any type of covering or enhancement that could cause people to judge me in any way. I quit dancing, gained the "freshman fifteen," and began rolling out of bed and heading to class exactly as I was. I cut off my permed and frosted hair and tossed my makeup, and instead of being enthusiastic and perky, which were my normal, natural traits, I intentionally cultivated a personality that was free of personality.

Which did not allow me to be seen authentically any more than wearing a bikini to choir had. Instead, it caused me to disconnect so completely from everything that had ever brought me joy that I lost all sense of who I was or what I liked. My quest for transparency led me straight into nothingness. Without any cover, who was I, and what could I possibly be worth?

Learning to Accessorize

Unsure of who I was or what I wanted, I quit school and moved home. As summer was drawing to a close and I still had zero idea who I was supposed to be, a friend called me in a panic. One of the girls on her university's pom squad had dropped out, and they needed one more dancer for camp the following week. My inner compass locked in immediately. My direction had found me! I wanted to dance, and I wanted to go back to college.

I was going to quit covering and judging myself, quit seeking approval and being embarrassed for who I was and what I found important. I was going to stop worrying about what other people might think. I was going to show my body, my brains, and my beliefs *my* way. I was going to build *my* dreams and live *my* sparkle. I was ready, and I couldn't wait to dive in!

This is how I uncovered myself, found my sparkle, and, for the first time in my life, released judgment about who I was — who I thought I was supposed to be — and stepped fully into my Naked Self-Worth. This is how I came back to life, challenged myself with every opportunity I could find, and ended up going to law school. Nothing was going to stop me now!

My Adulthood: The Power Woman in the Conservatively Cut Navy-Blue Business Suit

Nothing was going to stop me...except myself. I wish I could say that I remained so connected to who I was that I was never undone by my inhibitions or self-judgment again, but that was not the case. Which is why *FLAUNT!* is a practice to be gently but vigilantly embodied throughout our lives. In order to transcend our stories, to become the kind of women we aspire to be instead of the kind of women created by default by the sum total of our masks, we must stay vigilant. We must reveal ourselves fully and allow ourselves to be seen. And most importantly, we must abide by our own internal valuation system.

During my last year of law school, I was accepted in the university's student-law office, a program where students represent low-income clients under the supervision of licensed attorneys. In one of my cases, I represented a couple who purchased a used car from a dealership but quit making payments when the wife lost her job. Although my advisor and I had gone through the entire case file, the night before the hearing I went back to the law library to do some more research. Just in case.

Poring over case law, I discovered that there were various notice requirements the dealership had to fulfill before repossessing the car, and those notice requirements had not been met.

You probably know how it feels when you have a secret that is so joyful and thrilling that you can barely sleep? That's how I felt! I had found something that had been missed by everyone. I was ecstatic! I was going to win the very first case I had ever tried!

The next morning, even though I had barely slept, I put on my best (only) conservatively cut navy-blue suit, spent an hour on understated yet elegant hair and makeup, and made sure that I had all the necessary research and files. Beaming, I entered the courtroom with my advisor and presented both opposing counsel and the judge with a memo explaining what I had found.

After a couple of tense minutes, the judge banged his gavel and ruled in favor of my clients, who gave a whoop of joy as I broke into a relieved smile. I had done it! Looking up, I caught the judge's eye. He pointed straight at me and said, "I want to see you in my chambers *now!*" And he was not smiling.

Confused, I followed him to his chambers, where, instead of congratulating me, he berated me for unfairly springing my research on opposing counsel, an older, established (male) attorney, and for making him look ill prepared in court. He told me he didn't like the way I was all smiles with my clients. He explained that if I wanted to be taken seriously, I should wear pants, instead of a skirt. He also suggested I wear my hair up.

Have you ever had an experience that was so shocking that you didn't even know how to respond? Frozen to my advisor's side, I stood, incredulous. My smackdown was not the only source of my dismay. I was floored at the way my advisor respectfully kowtowed to the judge to his face, but later, outside his chambers, told me how out of line and flat-out wrong he had been. I drove home, mortified and confused, not registering for several hours that I had won my first case and should be proud of what I had accomplished.

If you have ever worked or played in traditionally more male-dominated arenas, you may have been confronted with the same decision I was: to play by the rules, fit in with the good old boys, and succeed or to be your true self and risk losing out on the career that you rightfully deserve. Because I wanted to succeed, I covered, going deeper and deeper into my female-lawyer persona, cutting off my hair and trying not to smile or connect with support staff the way I wanted. But in the process, I disconnected from myself. From my passion for justice, my body, and my love of dance and movement. I disconnected from my intuition; from my bubbly enthusiasm for, oh, *everything*; and, most profoundly, from my innate, feminine self.

Instead of being the lawyer I wanted to be, one who compassionately helped clients find solutions and solve problems outside the courtroom, I kept myself firmly in check and became the kind of traditional, detached, *see-you-in-court* lawyer others thought I should be. Once again I began dancing choreography that was not my own, wearing the costumes that fit the stereotypical version of the role I was playing, and masking who I was inside to avoid being rejected or hurt. And although I was successful, my success was not fulfilling. I had everything I could desire both professionally and personally, but something was missing. And I wasn't sure what it was or what I should do to find what I was looking for.

Aprons & Pearls, Spit-Up & Sweats

The birth of my second child brought with it the realization that I was being lied to. By both society and myself. Society told me that women could indeed do it all. All I had to do was lean in, be bold about taking on more at work, structure my time with my children clearly, and be proactive about planning date nights and self-care, and the world would be mine! But the truth is, no woman — let me rephrase that, *no human* — can sustain that level of superwoman intensity, constantly managing, planning, and rushing around, without sacrificing herself and her experience and enjoyment of life. Instead of questioning the message fed to me by society, I'd perceived myself as the failure, and I was done living that lie.

The situation was exacerbated by the fact that I was going on my third year without sleep, and I was suddenly disillusioned with my role as a powerful career woman who could do it all. I wanted more time with my children, and I was unhappy leaving them at daycare. Even though staying home hadn't been my plan and everyone thought I was crazy for "throwing away" my career and becoming a "lowly" wife and mom, I wanted to do it.

On a wave of conviction and coffee, I entered full-time motherhood, where I believed I would be welcomed with open arms into the mythic sisterhood of stay-at-home moms. I could while away the hours, babies playing happily at my feet, reconnecting with myself and shedding the layers I had accumulated during my time as an attorney. In reality, I stepped squarely onto the bloody fields of the mommy wars, where competition, self-judgment, and guilt threatened to overtake me at every turn.

The working moms were judgmental of the stay-at-home moms; the stay-at-home moms were judgmental of the working moms. Not everyone was willing to talk about the frustration and exhaustion of raising babies and toddlers. In fact, women who spoke freely about their bad parenting moments would sometimes be ostracized or, worse, be condescendingly told by the perfect mothers, "All you have to do is..."

Those perfect women — you might know the type — wearing a June Cleaver apron (or Athleta yoga gear) and carrying a tray of organic zucchini muffins, surrounded by their perfect children and bunco-club friends, all the while prattling on about their *ah-mazing* date night with their adoring hubby, made it seem like once again, I was two steps behind, an impostor in my own life.

What was wrong with me that I sometimes missed the peace of being at work, or my kids could make me want to run from the house screaming? I don't know if you can relate, but I felt like no matter how hard I tried, I could never be that perfect wife and mom. Which I found unbelievable, because I had been so capable on the work front! How was it possible to fail at being a stay-at-home mom?

This is how I lost myself to motherhood.

CHAPTER 2

Your Turn in the Spotlight!

*Y*ou've read my stories, you've seen the metaphoric masks and costumes I covered myself with. Now let's look at yours! Even though you know your stories, because you *lived* them, I challenge you to make each of them into a burlesque routine!

Say what, Lora?

Okay, here's how it works. Remember that burlesque is a parody! Dissociate from the emotion of what happened and focus on the lesson each story taught, the beliefs created, and the elaborate costumes and masks that were generated. See each memory, each story, as an episode in a miniseries, as a succession of interconnected burlesque routines that are the individual building blocks that helped create the woman you are today.

Creating a burlesque routine begins with a song, so strive to find one that personifies your story or sets the requisite mood. Hear that song as the background track to that memory and see if it reframes things. Next, move on to costuming. Since you are the star of your story, what are you wearing? Maybe not literally but symbolically. And what are the layers of this costume? What's being shown, and what's underneath, hidden? Are things being layered on or taken off? Again, reframe your memories and stories as routines, and see how the understanding surrounding that memory changes. Don't forget that jewelry, makeup, hair, and props are all part of costuming as well! What accessories are you wearing, and what do they symbolize? Last, what is the choreography, the order of action? How are you the star of your own routine?

Think of my stories, hear the ZZ Top song "Legs," and see me pom-pom-dancing around in a denim miniskirt, ruffle ankle socks, heels, and a *Flashdance*-inspired sweatshirt. But as I remove my sexy sweatshirt, notice the tightly laced corset, signifying my need for approval, that I reveal underneath. See how I trade a mask of bold, "can't hurt me" confidence for my lavender smart-girl glasses? As I unlace the corset, do you see my tender heart, which may be represented by soft-pink heart-shaped pasties? You get the idea! Have fun with this!

As you burlesque your own life, your own stories, recognize the constraints and inhibitions present there and in your way of thinking. See the impact society, family, friends, culture, religion, or your career had on you and your beliefs. Then turn those beliefs or constraints into a physical object that you can remove as you would a jacket, revealing the kind of woman you are underneath. The kind of woman you are in your heart, the woman you've always been. The woman you've always wanted others to really see.

It's like stepping into a virtual dressing room where you can try on — or take off — a wide variety of options and beliefs to see how they might look and feel before deciding to buy.

Don't be nervous — this is more like playing dress-up

than shopping for jeans! This is not about bashing everything valuable and meaningful, throwing away advice from everyone who has ever loved you or had your best interest at heart. These exercises and practices are to increase your level of awareness around who you are and why you do what you do. They help you recognize where your beliefs may have originated and give you the opportunity to try something new, to flaunt and expose yourself in ways you may never have dreamed!

Creating Your Costumes & Masks

For many of us, the story of our life begins long before we are even aware it's being written. And although this prewritten story is one that is appropriate for the beliefs of our culture and community, it may not be appropriate for us. From the moment we are born, we are labeled as a boy or a girl; taught how boys and girls should look, act, and feel; and judged as either capable or not. We are told what religion we are; what we should believe, value, and accept in life; and what we should expect from others. We form an identity based on what others tell us we should be, not necessarily on who we really are.

If we are smart, our families and teachers plot out a life of academic success, culminating in a prominent career. If we cry easily, we may be presented with a script that casts us as overly emotional, weak, or in need of protection. If we are a certain race or religion, we are handed scripts that include a lineage of persecution, limitation, privilege, or success.

We are taught what to expect from people of various cultures, religions, classes, genders, and political affiliations based on their label or stereotype, rather than our own firsthand knowledge or experience. While learning generalities about groups presents us with potentially useful information that guides our interactions, it also sets us up for misinterpretation and a tendency to judge others. Perhaps you can remember a time when you judged someone incorrectly, based on their label or stereotype? Uh-huh. I certainly can!

When the world, or the people in it, look different from the way we think they should, we become anxious, experiencing what is known as *cognitive dissonance.* Cognitive dissonance is the mental discomfort that occurs when our beliefs or assumptions are contradicted by new information. Whether this discomfort is major or minor, personal or impersonal, it is resolved in one of three ways. We either reject, explain away, or avoid information, in an attempt to persuade ourselves that no conflict really exists.

Growing up with an accountant for a father and a mother who worked part-time so she could stay at home with me meant that I was raised with some pretty conservative beliefs around money. Namely, that we did not spend what we did not have, and the only debt that was justifiable was a home mortgage. Period. For right or for wrong, that was my belief, and it served me well. Until law school.

There was no way I could ever save enough to pay for law school up front, and the only way that I could go was to take out student loans. Which, according to my childhood belief, was not justifiable debt. Cognitive dissonance! My assumption that only one kind of debt was valid failed to take into consideration that there could be a time and a place for debt, and that leveraging oneself in pursuit of an education could be a smart thing to do. Reject, explain away, or avoid. Those were my options.

Rejecting that belief would have made me stressed and scared, feeling like an irresponsible spendthrift. Avoiding the decision was not possible, since I desperately wanted to go to law school. So I explained it away in the most rationally irrational way possible. I took out student loans with the plan that a few years later when I bought a house, I would take out a larger loan and pay off my student loans with the extra mortgage-loan money! That way I would be left with only *justifiable* debt — a mortgage. And I did! See what I did there? That was a pretty sneaky way of fooling myself into being able to hold both my belief that *all debt except mortgage debt is bad* and still take out the student loans that I needed.

Cognitive dissonance has nothing to do with our level of education or intelligence. It's a universal phenomenon everyone experiences, and it's difficult to combat, because often we aren't consciously aware that we're engaging in it!

One Million and Fifty Shades of Glitter

Have you ever seen someone toss a handful of glitter into the air, either under bright stage lights or in sunlight? It's beautiful, glorious — and distracting! Why? Because the glitter reflects and refracts the light, causing us to take our eyes off whatever is happening onstage and focus instead on the scintillating shimmer of distraction all around. Which is exactly what happens in our own lives. We get distracted by others, by our own thoughts, ideas, and personal histories. Pretty soon we don't know what's real and what's the glittery distraction of cognitive dissonance.

The upcoming exercise, called "Living in the Glitter," consists of eleven questions for you to use to uncover your own cognitive dissonance. They help you see if your beliefs are based on reality or if you are rejecting, explaining away, or avoiding new information in order to keep your assumptions intact.

Let me give you an example of what this might look like: I have a client who was raised with the belief that homosexuality is a sin. Unbeknownst to her, one of her best friends growing up was gay. As you might imagine, when he revealed that he was gay and asked her to attend his wedding, it was like a cloud of glitter had suddenly been tossed into her brain. How could she attend the wedding and support her friend in his happiness while also maintaining her belief that homosexuality is a sin? She couldn't wrap her head around how he could simultaneously be a *sinner* and the *spiritual, wonderful human being* she knew him to be. No matter which way she looked, glittery confusion reigned. Resolving this conflict meant she could:

(a) reject her belief that homosexuality is a sin, potentially setting herself at odds with the beliefs of her church, family, and other loved ones;

(b) avoid both the wedding and her firsthand knowledge and experience confirming her friend's high-quality character and deep spiritual connectedness, possibly resulting in the termination of their friendship; or

(c) find a way to explain why both her conflicting beliefs could be true. In this instance, she rationalized that her friend and his partner were the one *exception* to the otherwise accurate belief that homosexuality is sinful, thus allowing her to attend and celebrate their wedding with joy and still hold both contradictory beliefs comfortably.

Cognitive dissonance — otherwise known as hypocritical behavior — allows us to maintain our belief system, ensures our survival, and makes us feel good about being a hypocritical, contradictory mess! Don't fret; we're all this way.

In looking at your own stories, can you identify where cognitive dissonance may have crept in? Probably not easily, which is why, before delving into the stories of your childhood, adolescence, and early adulthood, we begin with the "Living in the Glitter" exercise. These filter questions provide new context and insight for the key moments and stories that affected you along the way. They help you challenge your own long-standing beliefs and put you in touch with your own hypocritical messiness so you can see your cognitive dissonance for what it is: a way to reject, explain away, or avoid anything that challenges the veracity of your beliefs.

Black, White & Glitter

Have you noticed that most of life is neither black nor white but some scintillating shade of glitter that you can't quite name? One moment it looks gold, then the light catches it and it's red, but then a silver fleck jumps into view. If you have ever listed out pros and cons to help you make decisions and then still not been able to decide, you will know exactly what I'm talking about. Wouldn't life be easier if everything was just cut-and-dried? Look at how frequently news stories deal with elusive, shimmery shades of glitter. Did the officer shoot the suspect because he posed a viable danger and the officer feared for his life, or did he act unreasonably based on a racial bias? Whoa. Is this something we can ever answer with complete certainty? Probably not, and that uncertainty can be excruciating.

The discomfort that comes from living in this glittery confusion sometimes makes us want to pretend that things are clear and precise, even when they are not. Instead of admitting that life is filled with value judgments, errors, and complexities none of us could ever see through, we sometimes pretend that we can. And in slipping back into our black-and-white ways of thinking and reacting, we overlook the fact that sometimes, it is in the glittery, complex tragedies that the biggest gains and unexpected joys are born.

What are some of the black-and-white beliefs held by your family? If you are looking for a starting point, think about the biggies: race, gender, nationality, religion, marital status, political affiliation, level of education, and sexual orientation. But know that it's usually the subtle ones, like *A worthy woman sacrifices for her family* that are more impactful.

Reading my story about student loans and my conviction that having debt was not okay, you probably won't be surprised that one of the black-and-white beliefs held by my family was that wasting things (especially money) was wrong. Like really, really wrong. The energy crisis of the seventies was in full swing during my childhood, inflation and mortgage interest were on the rise, and my parents were living on one income.

The principle of *not wasting* is neither right nor wrong, black nor white. It simply is. However, my family's black-and-white belief affected me, causing me cognitive dissonance around money and my own spending habits. I felt the need to justify my expenditures to myself, classifying all expenses as frugal, so as not to be wasteful and wrong. But the fact was, most of the decisions I made about money were neither frugal nor wasteful. They were just decisions!

Using the "Living in the Glitter" filter questions, I was able to see where I rejected the notion that being wasteful was okay, explained away why I needed to spend what I did, and avoided being honest about my spending or budgeting. I came to terms with the fact that I could be both frugal and wasteful at the same time and integrated new information and beliefs around money into my life, making me much happier and easier to live with. And since glitter is an all-season color, let's embrace the glitter!

· ● ● ● ·

Living in the Glitter

Ask yourself these filter questions, and see what shifts for you. Move through the questions with a sense of curiosity and wonderment, as if you were watching a burlesque routine (*Ohhhh, I can't wait to see what's underneath that!*), instead of with blame, shame, or judgment.

1. Besides me, who around me holds this belief?
2. Is there a reason that I, or those around me, hold this belief?

     Let me butt in for a moment here and explain what I mean by a *reason* for holding a certain belief. My grandpa was a pilot in both World War II and the Korean War. His experience, coupled with wartime propaganda, shaped his beliefs about those of Asian descent. A reason is not a justification. It does not excuse the belief or make it correct. It explains logically why someone would feel the way that they do. And until we discover those reasons, we are much less likely to create lasting change.

3. How is my belief true?
4. What evidence can I find that supports my belief, and what is the quality of this evidence?

     Okay, okay, the preceding question is a tad lawyerly and a little ridiculous, I admit. It's just that there *may* have been a time or two when I was more interested in being right than in really, honestly being *right*. And I *may* have gone to great lengths to *prove* a position that in my heart and head I knew wasn't accurate. Mum's the word. Perhaps you can relate.

5. How is my belief false?
6. What evidence can I find that is contrary to my belief, and what is the quality of that evidence?
7. Does this contradiction cause me mental angst or discomfort?

8. In what ways have I rejected this contradictory evidence?
9. In what ways have I attempted to explain away this contradictory evidence?
10. In what ways have I avoided looking at this contradictory evidence?
11. What would changing my belief mean for me, as well as for my relationships with others?

As you walk through the rest of this chapter and the next one, see if you can identify beliefs that arose as a consequence of your childhood stories.

Maybe it's time you slipped into something a bit more comfortable?

· · · · · • • • ● ● ● ● ● • • • · ·

How Black-and-White Thinking
Leads to Self-Judgment

Living without conscious exploration of our programmed beliefs can trap us in a cycle of self-judgment that robs us of our ability to be seen for who we really are. It can also prevent us from fully growing up and creating our own independent identity. Instead of looking objectively at ourselves, building upon our strengths and healthily exposing our weaknesses, we create a facade. While that facade may protect us from criticism or from having to look too deep within ourselves and square our own contradictory beliefs, when we fail to reconcile our external persona with who we are on the inside, we end up engaging in an elaborate game of hide-and-seek that has long-term unhealthy consequences. When we cover parts of our true selves that are out of alignment with the persona we have created, we lie about — and discount the veracity of — our internal world in favor of an artificial construct. We fail to establish our own well-thought-out identity, independent of the wounds, vulnerabilities, and neuroses of others.

And as a consequence, we can never truly be seen or accepted. Either by ourselves or by others.

Contradictory Contradictions

Living in the glitter means being self-aware about the conflicting and contradictory areas of your life. Knowing that certain things about you don't make sense and being okay anyway. It's like admitting that you are a vegetarian who sometimes delights in a good, juicy burger.

Having awareness of our contradictory beliefs decreases the amount of internal stress that we experience, because it provides space for both the conflict and the solution. Internal discord comes from covering up (lying about) our periodic passion for burgers because it appears to be in conflict with our concurrent belief that vegetarianism is both healthier and a more environmentally sustainable way to live. Our beliefs don't have to make perfect sense! When we are aware of our own contradictions, it means that we no longer feel compelled to lie to ourselves, our internal discord decreases, and we feel peace.

Holding contradicting beliefs isn't the problem; pretending that our beliefs are always perfectly rational and noncontradictory is the problem. The fact that we aren't neat little packages of culinary ideology — or anything else, for that matter — is not alarming. Nobody is that black-and-white about anything. What is alarming is the way we habitually lie to ourselves and to others, covering who we are and what we believe.

This habitual covering is so ingrained in us and our society that we don't even realize we are doing it. Act I of this book is all about recognizing and releasing this covering. And since the thing that holds us back is often an unexamined belief or idea that has been a part of us since childhood, it can be difficult for us to see. Our subconscious minds and our childhood programming, in particular, are like the main operating system of a computer. The operating system runs all our various programs, and while we are aware of the various programs that are running, we are usually not aware of the main operating system until it interferes with those programs. Our own unexamined beliefs tend to stay really hidden, until we try to maneuver around them.

Which is why storytelling is so impactful to humans. Because we more easily see lessons through others than we do through ourselves. Not sure what I mean? Think of the parables of the Bible, the lessons in Aesop's fables, or the lore of nursery rhymes. If someone accuses me of being needlessly dramatic, calling for help where none is necessary, I might become defensive or not fully comprehend. But tell me a story about a shepherd *crying wolf*, and I totally get it. Humans learn through story.

You know my coming-of-age stories and the ideas and beliefs that were formed as a result. Now let's reflect on yours. But before we do, allow me to give you a friendly little warning about what to expect in the rest of Act I. Chapters 2 and 3 are the deepest, most introspective portions of the whole book, encouraging you to unearth the stories of your childhood, adolescence, and adulthood and reexamine them through a new and different lens. Use the "Living in the Glitter" filter questions to challenge your own long-standing beliefs and assumptions so you can be free to re-choreograph your life according to who you are today. Please do not read everything in one sitting! Break it down. Work through the stories of your child-hood and stop. Allow yourself some time to ponder and reflect. Tackle your adolescence, then take a break. Move on to your adulthood when you feel ready. Allow yourself the grace and space to let this process unfold naturally, to trip the light fan-tastic and to really *enjoy*, without rushing toward Act II.

Your Childhood Wardrobe: Begin with a Classic Base Layer of Self-Judgment...

As odd as it might sound to those of us who were raised by parents who said things like, "If all your friends jumped off a cliff, would you jump off, too?" one of the first things we teach children is how to compare and judge themselves against external standards. Instead of cultivating intrinsic motivation and self-satisfaction, our society layers on external rules and teaches children that their worth is based on how well they please others. Crazy? You betcha!

As young children, before our indoctrination into "who we are supposed to be" and "what we are supposed to do" is com-plete, we generally had no problem being exactly who we were, without shame or judgment. Whether we were shy and with-drawn or bold and daring, we had no problem showing it. We were unapologetic about what we liked or what we thought, and it wasn't our concern if somebody else saw things differ-ently. We were honest about who we were, and we were curious about life. If we were curious about something new and dif-ferent, we approached it, seeking more. If we were frightened by something new and different, we announced our fear, hid our heads, or cried. Instead of pretending, judging ourselves, or making excuses, we expressed what we felt.

Before our childhood indoctrination, we lived out our truth, whether that truth was socially acceptable or not. If we wanted to color outside the lines, we did so with joyful abandon. We had no judgments about which toys were "appropriate"; we just knew what we liked, or explored freely until we did. We were unselfconscious and nonjudgmental, flaunting ourselves, laughing out loud, and smearing spaghetti in our hair simply to feel what spaghetti in the hair might feel like. We did not feel guilty for touching our bodies, sleeping in too late, or eating what we pleased, nor did we attempt to change ourselves based on the opinions of others.

We navigated our lives moment by moment, going from the jungle gym to the sandbox to the slides, with very few concerns. We didn't try to contain our own emotions, and we comfortably expressed whatever we felt without embarrassment, judgment, or shame. Above all, we trusted that each day was designed especially for us, because as the center of our own universe, we deemed ourselves worthy of such magic.

And since we were not influenced much by the opinions of others, we were difficult to control.

Wise parents and caregivers who wanted us to succeed in life looked for ways to control us and to influence our behavior, guiding, socializing, and introducing us, step-by-step, into society. Boys may have had dolls taken out of their arms and been told, "You don't want people to see you playing with a girl toy, do you?" Girls may have been told not to get dirty or play wild, "like a boy."

But no matter what we were taught, the bottom line was, if we were good girls, who did what we were supposed to do, we would be rewarded; and if we were bad girls, who disobeyed, we would be punished. We were taught that disobeying the rules would hurt those around us and make us feel bad. We were taught that our obedience would please those around us, bringing us pride, joy, and satisfaction.

Let that sink in. We were taught to have shame. We were taught to judge ourselves. We were taught that other people's opinions of us were more important than our own opinion of ourselves. In order to make us easier to control and easier to teach.

We were conditioned to believe that we could control other people's happiness through our actions: "Don't make Daddy mad by crying!" or "You will make Mommy so proud if you clean your plate!" What an enormous burden to carry! No wonder, as adults, we still believe that our obedience or conformity has earth-shattering implications for those around us. Perhaps, like me, you are so conditioned to please, to think that things can't be done correctly unless you are involved, that you sometimes have a hard time saying no. Many of us, no matter how educated or self-aware, still fall into this type of good-girl, people-pleasing syndrome, believing we can make others happy if only we try harder!

It is important to learn the beautiful traditions of our culture, our family heritage, and how to keep ourselves safe, healthy, and fun to be around. It is essential to know how to behave in public, respect others, and defer to authority. It's just that, for many of us, the balance between learning to please and respect others…and learning to please and respect ourselves got lost. Many of us inadvertently learned to deny our emotions, condemn ourselves for our natural tendencies, and adopt the mindset that who we are, at our core, is defective or wrong. Because much of our learning consisted of suppressing our individuality, bringing it more in line with those around us by avoiding the things that could lead to shame or embarrassment, we grew accustomed to covering and hiding essential pieces of our personality.

No matter how we were raised, many of us still equate our

inherent goodness, or badness, with the feedback we receive from others. It is from this place of guilt and shame that we learn that, in order to be successful, we need to judge ourselves stringently against external standards, always striving to do more, because otherwise we will never be good enough.

This classic base layer of childhood indoctrination, woven from shame, fear, and judgment and stitched together with a healthy dose of "or else," is the garment many of us have worn close to our hearts for so long that we may not even be aware that it's there. We spend the rest of our lives mired in self-judgment, shame, and the subtle feeling of unworthiness, without knowing why.

When we *FLAUNT!* we strip out of this base layer, and we set ourselves free.

· • ● • ·

Field Trip: "I'll Tell You What I Want, What I Really, Really Want"

As adults, many of us have no idea what we want. Especially high achievers. Those of us who move competently into our heads, successfully performing tasks and fulfilling our responsibilities to a T. Those of us who are adept at doing all that we "must" do in order to succeed often forget how to move into our hearts, tune in to ourselves, and articulate what we want. We get so conditioned to responding with the "right" answer that we forget to answer with the truth.

I'm guessing that, like most kids, at times you covered your beliefs, went along with popular opinion, and pretended to like something you didn't. Or perhaps you tried to impress another by being someone you weren't. Maybe you didn't want to be perceived as difficult or rock the boat. Or maybe it was because you weren't really sure *what* you wanted.

Although we all have different childhood experiences, for this exercise I want you to go back to a place and time when you were naked, before you learned to cover and hide yourself, to remember everything that brought your heart and soul pure, creative joy. You know, before socialization and indoctrination kicked in! This exercise focuses on the fun, positive, and creative aspects of play. You are not digging into trauma; you're digging into joy, and you are doing it by taking a field trip!

Think of places you enjoyed as a child and, like a good caregiver would, plan a field trip for yourself so you can reconnect with play and the activities that brought you joy. If you loved playing with toys and using your imagination to create elaborate scenarios, plan a field trip to the most captivating toy store you can find. The reason for this exercise is to reexperience how you felt playing, using your senses to explore toys, so get out there and experience play! If you loved dolls, go to the dolls. If you were into games, peruse the games.

Look at the toys. Notice their colors and packaging. Pick them up and see how they feel in your hands. Touch them. Feel their texture and weight. Smell them. Do you remember the scent of doll hair, crayons, or glue? Listen to the sounds they make and remember how you played. What story lines would you create? Imagine taking a boat in the bathtub with you now. Would you sail it around, plunging it in and out of the water? Is it a struggle to remember how to play and what to do?

Move to a section that is unfamiliar to you. If you were never into sports, check out the sporting goods, or head over to cars, trucks, and *boy toys*. Is there anything you might want to try out now that you did not explore as a child? With fresh eyes, wander around the store and imagine how to play with the different toys. Resist the urge to think about your kids, grandkids, nieces, nephews, or neighbors' kids. This is about you, not them! Yes, you are an adult. Play is out of your area of expertise, which is exactly the point! There are no societal rules or expectations regarding what toys an adult woman should or should not enjoy, so you are forced to drop into your heart, tune in to your desires, and figure it out — for you. Fly free, little bird!

On your way home, stop by a museum, park, playground, or beach. Play on the equipment, kick a ball, splash in the surf, or build sandcastles. Jump rope while chanting jump-rope songs in your head, play jacks, draw with sidewalk chalk, blow bubbles, or go down the slide. Anything works as long as it gets you back in your own body!

As you play, notice what comes up. Is it difficult for you to relax or to move unselfconsciously? Feeling awkward is both normal and good for us, as it stimulates the body and builds new neural pathways. Do you feel silly or bored, like you are wasting your time, or does playing make you secretly happy? Is the whole concept of play difficult for you? Why? *Don't try to change your feelings; just notice them.* Notice the voices in your head as you play. Are they yours, or do they originate from somewhere else? *This is silly* and *I'm too old for this* are good examples. Where did these judgments come from? Perhaps you hear your father telling you to "grow up and do something productive with your time" or your brother telling you that "only babies play with dolls"?

Many adults feel awkwardness, shame, or judgment around play. Get in touch with those feelings. The reason we play like a kid instead of playing like a grown-up and doing wine Wednesday or going to bunco is because we already know the rules and expectations surrounding *how* to do wine Wednesday or play bunco. There are no rules or expectations around how grown-ups should play with toys, so we have to relax, get out of our heads, and let our creativity flow. Which is actually beneficial for our professional lives as well. So, if you are having trouble getting into the groove, remind yourself that building with Legos or playing with dolls just might be good for your career!

And you know what? If this experience falls totally flat for you, that's fine, too. Playing is kind of a big stretch for those of us who have been living in our heads, disconnected from our bodies and imaginations for too long. *FLAUNT!* is a practice just like yoga or meditation, and if you are anything like me, sometimes you just can't get in the groove right away. And there's nothing wrong with that.

· · · · · • • ● ● ● ● ● ● • • · · · · ·

...Add on Some Stereotypical Hand-Me-Downs

In addition to the base layer of self-judgment that keeps us judging ourselves relentlessly throughout our adulthood, many of us inherited a boxful of biases, or lenses, that we use to view others. And like the metaphorical box of hand-me-down clothing, sometimes those lenses and biases are a perfect fit and sometimes they aren't. As kids we were taught to stereotype and judge others, not because those around us were narrow-minded bigots, but in order to help us live expediently and stay safe in our society. Black-and-white is always easier to teach than the infinite shades of glitter!

Stereotyping is nothing more than an efficient classification system that allows humans to more easily identify threats. Just as the spots on a butterfly's wings that look like eyes deter predators, who sort and classify which prey is worth hunting and which is not, so do humans sort and classify other humans based on what they see. The problem is, like the butterfly or the box of hand-me-down lenses, sometimes it creates an illusion.

Cultures throughout history have used some sort of classification system — whether through tattoos, scars, jewelry, piercings, clothing, headdresses, or accessories — to identify different roles and levels of status within their society. In our own culture we use uniforms to identify police, firefighters, and medical professionals. Men in uniforms are good and can be trusted, but men with shaved heads, piercings, and tattoos cannot. And men wearing priest's collars are pious men of God with whom we can entrust our children.

While we are raised to believe that we can tell a lot about a person just by looking at them, as we know, people don't follow all aspects of the roles they play, any more than we fit all aspects of the roles we play. Stereotyping others based on their role or label is a viable way to increase our efficiency and keep us safe, but it is not foolproof. Ignoring the fallibility of the tools we use keeps us locked in a black-and-white, all-or-nothing mindset that the world has a duty to conform to our personal stereotypes and preconceived notions.

When others don't match up to our preconceived belief about who they should be — instead of realizing we have made an incorrect assumption, that we are viewing them through a hand-me-down lens — we sometimes claim that *they* are wrong for not fitting into *our* views! Look at Ted Bundy. Like his victims, I would probably be pretty taken with his looks, intelligence, and charm, scoffing at the idea that someone like him could be a dangerous killer. What about Mother Teresa? If you didn't know who she was, might you dismiss her as being some insignificant old foreign lady? Scary, isn't it?

In the same way we inadvertently learned to meet the expectations of others, instead of meeting *ours*, so too did we inadvertently learn to judge others based on their stereotype rather than on the information at hand. Instead of being taught how to differentiate people from their labels, roles, and scripts, we viewed them with our hand-me-down lenses and beliefs, plugging them into the confines of the roles we had in mind for them, feeling disappointment, anger, or disillusionment when they failed to live up to our stereotypical misapprehension of who and what they should be.

Beneath the Mask

Meditation and hypnotherapy are two sides of the same coin. They both describe normal and natural states of consciousness that all humans move into and out of several times a day, and they both provide access to the subconscious (also known as the unconscious) mind. The difference is that meditation focuses on the absence of thoughts, perceptions, or reactions, whereas hypnosis is a focused state of heightened awareness, perception, and learning. Meditation is more of an unstructured journey into a state of mindful relaxation, and hypnosis is a well-structured journey with specific goals in mind.

After our field trip, where we reconnected with our ability to play, our minds are primed and ready to reignite some of the joy that was touched upon as we set aside expectation and allowed ourselves to experience each moment as it came. The following Magical Meditation facilitates creativity and provides space for our minds to wander and unearth whatever is buried in our hearts.

Magical Meditation

Find a comfortable place to relax where you won't be disturbed. Take a few breaths, and allow yourself to settle in the moment and whatever that moment is bringing. If you are distracted or uncomfortable, allow yourself to be distracted and uncomfortable.

Release all thoughts of what meditation should feel like and just be where you are.

On your next inhalation, breathe in the thoughts you are thinking or the emotions you are feeling. Exhale whatever it is you are thinking or feeling.

Be here as long as you need, until you have breathed in and then breathed out all unsatisfying thoughts and emotions, and are left breathing in and breathing out only thoughts and emotions that are pleasant to you.

From this state of pure satisfaction, fill yourself with a sense of playful positivity, where anything is possible, and just be.

When you are ready, imagine, visualize, or pretend that you are a tiny, beautiful baby or a beautiful, luminescent soul, floating on a cloud, waiting to descend to Earth and begin your life. But before your life on Earth, you have been given the opportunity to review the dreams, desires, gifts, and passions that form your core essence, the sparkly center of your innate being.

What are your dreams and desires? How will you use your gifts and pursue your passions? Why is your soul here now? What is your life mission, and when your life is finally over, what will your legacy be? Will you be satisfied with this life?

Breathe, relax, and let your mind wander into this creative, joyful space.

Without judgment toward yourself or others, and knowing that all things happen for a reason and in perfect order, notice how your life has moved both toward and away from your dreams, desires, passions, and gifts. There is no judgment, because, like the path of a labyrinth, life moves us both toward and away from ourselves and our goals.

Notice the parts of your inner core, your true essence, that have been covered. Your masks, stories, and costumes. But most importantly, notice what lies beneath those masks. Watch as everything that is not your true essence, everything that is a story or mask or judgment, slowly crumbles and falls away, and feel yourself smile.

As you allow the unmasking.

As stories that are not your own fall away.

And allow your dreams, desires, passions, and gifts to be reignited by this noticing.

What does life look like, now that you have an awareness of what lies beneath your costumes and masks and what your inner core is made from; and now that your dreams, desires, gifts, and passions are smoldering, on the brink of catching fire?

Notice where your life is leading.

When you feel ready, slowly let your mind move back to the present, back in your body. Take three or four deep breaths, preparing for the day or night ahead, staying connected to your own creative insight, divine possibility, and uninhibited joy.

There's no right or wrong way to experience this or any meditation. Like you did during your field trip to the toy store, step back and see what happens. Notice where your mind goes. Be surprised by your dreams and desires, your passions and purpose, and by the legacy you desire to leave. If you found it difficult to stay focused during your own meditation and would like to try a guided meditation led by yours truly, then head over to loracheadle.com/freebies and download my free MP3 "Finding Your Passion & Purpose."

Viewing your life as a whole, from a detached, higher perspective, validates the longings of your inner being and gives you the opportunity to start fresh, to push the reset button on your life. Even though you can't control everything that happens in life, you can always control your response to what happens. Resetting yourself back to your original core is always the right choice!

· ● ● ● ·

Childhood Self-Reflection Stories

What were your childhood stories and experiences? Whether they are significant or fairly typical and unremarkable, they are still the experiences that made you who you are today. What were some of the hand-me-down lenses you were given to view others? What were the stories you wrote for others, perhaps unknowingly boxing them into your interpretation of who they ought to be?

Jot down three or four stories from your childhood that come to mind.

Identify the takeaway or beliefs that came from those stories; then go back to the filter questions from the "Living in the Glitter" exercise (pages 47–48) and see if challenging those beliefs produces any different results or affects what you believe today.

Finally, burlesque those stories up! Visualize what music might have been playing, what type of costume you could have worn, and in grand musical-theater style, what kind of dance you would have danced. How does burlesquing your memories reframe your past?

· · · · · · · ● ● ● ● ● ● ● · · · · · ·

Your Adolescent Adventures: Teenage Virtual Reality

Adolescence is a time of sorting and selecting, of pruning both the unused neural pathways and the unused portions of our identities, shaping our brains and our identities for adulthood.

While our childhood stories often involve being guided toward identities that our family and culture think are most appropriate for us, the stories of our teen years tend to involve some combination of conformity and rebellion as we establish our adult identity. Like playing an endless virtual-reality game, teens try on and sort through a wide variety of personalities and behaviors in an attempt to find out *who they really are*, separate from their family of origin.

It's during the teen years that many of us become aware of how big and broad the world truly is and how many options are available to us. While thrilling, this awareness can increase our anxiety about our "proper" role within that world. So too does our realization that our childhood identity is not fixed and that we are in the process of leaving behind the securely black-and-white world we knew so well. This double whammy leaves many of us unsure of what we are "supposed" to do, be, or even believe. While childhood teaches us to put everyone, including ourselves, into neat little boxes, adolescence teaches us that those boxes do not always work the way we've been taught. Which is scary!

As a result, we try out a random assortment of behaviors, sometimes clinging to that which was taught in childhood and other times casting off our childhood identity entirely and rebelling against everything we knew to be true. As our formerly black-and-white truth becomes a glittery mass of swirling color, we either hide it from others or unceremoniously shove our confusion and angst down the throats of our unsuspecting family. Adolescence is the first time we construct an identity independent of our families, potentially shutting down parts of ourselves in an attempt to be "just like everyone else." Which explains why peer pressure is so powerful during the adolescent years and why we watch others, hoping to get it right ourselves!

You may remember being a teen, gauging what you should do based on the behavior of others or feeling like everyone else had it all together, except you. You may remember feeling kind of nervous or even scared when you ran across someone who was *different*, who did not fit into the status quo. Perhaps you could relate to the pain of feeling like an outsider, and you sensed that if you were not careful, you, too, could end up that way. If you were anything like me, torn between being a really good girl and also wanting to have some fun, you may have acknowledged your deepest thoughts, feelings, and desires only to yourself, wasting an extraordinary amount of energy worrying, wondering, and covering up who you really were because you did not want others to suspect the confusion going on inside.

Have you ever noticed that those who are the most vocally opposed to certain behaviors on the outside are sometimes the ones who secretly embrace them on the inside? Like the outspoken politician who is adamant about family values yet gets caught up in the most salacious scandals? It is human nature to deflect attention away from the parts of us that we wish to keep hidden, and the quickest way to do that is to vehemently oppose that which we are trying to hide. If you have raised teenagers, then you probably know exactly what I'm talking about!

· **●** ● ● ·

Field Trip: "Poppin' Tags," Poppin' Personas

Once again, it's time to go on a field trip, but this time we are going to a thrift store! Like a virtual-reality game, you will create two different avatars, except instead of doing it virtually, you will do it in reality! Your mission is to find two outfits (*ahem*, burlesque costumes) that represent different aspects of who you are. The first one is who you are in your normal, everyday life. The second is your totally uninhibited, alter-ego, superwoman, inner-burlesque-star self, who powerfully embodies everything you love and all that lies deep in your core. This outfit is a literal altar to everything that are you. It's what I like to call your *altar* ego — a tribute or an altar to the most powerful, authentic parts of yourself. Remember the Magical Meditation, where you were on a cloud waiting to be born? Your *altar*-ego outfit represents the full expression of all that you were meant to be and all that you are.

This is burlesque! This is not supposed to be serious. Or subtle. You are making a parody or a caricature of both versions of yourself using clothing to convey the message of who you are to others. Create the most ridiculous version of yourself you can muster, and use your clothing and accessories to help you make this statement. It's sorta, kinda like reliving your teenage fashion mistakes without the fear of photos surfacing years later.

Speaking of photos, when you are in the dressing room, be sure to sneak a few selfies or snap some pictures of yourself in the dressing-room mirror in both outfits, and keep them for future reference. You will need them for an exercise in Act II. Or you can buy the things you find, which is actually pretty stinking fun. On that note, this exercise is ridiculously fun when done with a group of friends, a sister, a daughter, or even a partner. As we talked about earlier, oftentimes we see others more clearly than we see ourselves, and it's a riot to get others' perspective about what we should be wearing!

Begin by putting together the outfit that represents who you are now, the facade that you present to the world in your normal, everyday life. Look for over-the-top examples that instantly show others exactly who you are. If someone were to be you for Halloween, what would they wear? If you always wear stretchy leggings with long, flowing tops, find the most ridiculous example of *long, flowing top* that you can find. Love pink? Find pink jeans, pink socks, a pink purse, pink shoes, a pink top, and pink hair accessories.

This is the outfit that you wear as you symbolically come onstage. Which means it's also the outfit that you remove. What are the inhibitions you wish to release? Are you tired of holding on to body shame? What garments could symbolize this shame? Like me, did you feel like you were wearing a corset? If so, your outfit could include a *perfect-little-princess corset of perfection* that you could remove by slowly and deliberately unthreading the laces, one rivet at a time. As a power mom and former lawyer, I might also find a *conservatively cut navy-blue business suit*, but instead of clutching a briefcase, I might top it off with a cheesy diaper bag, running shoes, and athletic socks, since I teach fitness and am always *running* late.

Act I is about recognizing and releasing the parts of ourselves that we adopted in order to please others or fit it, and burlesque is the literal stripping away of those constraints. So find props or clothing that represent the inhibitions you wish to release, and allow yourself to strip them away! Releasing something tangible as you release on an emotional level is enormously powerful. Look for items that are meaningful to you. Cultural, religious, or familial icons are obvious examples, but you can be more symbolic or familiar, too. If your career was limited because you had to take over the family business whose logo was a cat, finding a cat stuffed animal or a T-shirt with a cat on it can be the perfect representation of that business.

Your second outfit, the one that's revealed when you take off your first, is your *altar* ego, everything you are deep inside. Your untapped potential. Your wild, free spirit and everything you have aspired to do or become. If your toy-store field trip reminded you of your childhood desire to be a princess or a pirate and that's the energy you wish to channel, now's your chance to create a grown-up version of that latent identity. Go to the formal dresses and pick out the most gloriously amazing number you can find. Or head to the men's section and move into your repressed masculine. Think of this as a vision board for your body. What would you wear if you were free to wear anything at all? Thrift stores are glorious treasure troves of possibility, and your job is to uncover those possibilities.

Find things you passionately love, things that make you giggle or feel deliciously naughty or unstoppably sexy and powerful! A rock star with a toy magic mic, a black leather coat, fishnets, and spike-studded stilettos? Perfect! A leopard-print robe, pink fuzzy slippers, sponge rollers, and a TV tray? Exactly right! A sleek yet conservative dress…fabulous. Did your parents, spouse, family, or friends — or a magazine article — once tell you that you couldn't, or shouldn't, wear something that you loved? Well, now's your chance!

Think back to the times you were out shopping and found something you loved but didn't buy because it wasn't practical. Either because you had no place to wear it, it was too expensive, or it just wasn't appropriate. Look for that thing now. Buy the dress, the shoes, the purse, or the funky plates with matching *Star Trek*–themed drinking glasses. Thrift stores are fun because they bring an element of whimsy, a spirit of adventure, and the opportunity to indulge in a crazy fantasy without commitment and without breaking the budget!

During one of my trips to the thrift store, I found the most gorgeous wedding dress, ever. It was unlike my own 1990s chiffon explosion, and it fit me like a glove. For some weird reason that I really can't explain, it made me feel beautiful, sexy, powerful, and chosen. So, for thirty-five dollars, I bought that fantasy. I told myself that someday I'd make it into a burlesque costume, but every time I pull it out and think about altering it, I choose not to.

Have you ever had something like that in your own closet? Something that you know you will never wear but you can't bring yourself to get rid of, either? Whether it's the memories or the potential it represents, it makes you feel good for a reason. That's the feeling you are going for here.

Don't put pressure on yourself to find, or to even know, what you are looking for. You can go back a few times, hit a variety of different thrift stores, or create whatever you envision on your own. Love the fake fur collar on one jacket and the sparkly logo on another? Buy them both, cut off the collar, and stitch or hot-glue it onto the jacket. This is not about being perfect; it's about having the gumption to create whatever you want to create, your way. The less perfect the better. Allow yourself the grace and the space to craft like a kindergartner if that's your level. It's my level, and it works fine for me!

This exercise is about the power of creating a living, breathing vision board of glittery burlesque deliciousness of yourself, both at your most powerful center and in your everyday persona. But it is also about how we can walk into a thrift store, not knowing what we are looking for — because we have no expectations — and have things that we love serendipitously fall right in our laps.

When we show up — without expectation, without preconceived notions of how to do it right, without seeking approval, judging ourselves every step of the way and worrying that we aren't good enough — when we quit fighting so hard and relax into the magic of infinite possibility, magic happens. So many of us get caught up in labels, stereotypes, rules, and reality. Remember that burlesque is not reality. Burlesque is a glorious, glittery, larger-than-life extravaganza that's thought-provoking and fun. Listen to your heart, to your altar ego. Find things that bring you joy, and play with those things. If mermaid is your jam, do mermaid, and do it your way.

Recognize, release, and reveal!

CHAPTER 3

Igniting & Integrating Your Sparkle

During our thrift-store excursion, we created two distinct identities in the space of a single morning or afternoon. In real life, our identities don't evolve that quickly. In any transformation, there are steps along the way, between points A and B, that facilitate the process. Typically, we don't just snap our fingers — or blink, like in *I Dream of Jeannie* — and change occurs. We evolve. We develop. We grow up. Sometimes our personal evolution makes perfect sense, and other times we wake up wondering, *How the heck did I end up here?*

Evolving Avatars

The growing-up process results in a wide variety of experiences, stories, and habits, some really good and others less than ideal. But either way, they are all our own. Are you in the habit of embracing all versions of yourself, or are you in the habit of striving to become something you aren't while denying all that you *were?* As tempting as it might be to ignore certain parts of our own evolution, shutting down vast sections of our identity — sections that, while not our current identity, still make up the sum total of who we are — doesn't work, either. Wherever we go, there we are! We must take all facets of who we are along with us if we expect to feel whole and complete. Even the parts that we have evolved through. Let me explain.

Some of the roles or identities we evolve into are those we've chosen or created, and some aren't. Some were thrust on us whether we were ready or not. Whatever the circumstances, the relevant question is whether we played those roles based on our full history or limited ourselves and adopted someone else's history. When we are in the habit of incorporating ourselves into our own lives, we bring our innate nature, our core self, and our vast life experience to all that we do. And we thrive. We stay energized, peaceful, and satisfied, because we remain connected to all that we are, and there is congruence between the inner and outer versions of ourselves, as well as between all versions we have ever been.

Feeling unworthy or insecure leads to the habit of disconnecting from our inner self and moving into a stereotypical version of who we think we should be, in order to protect our true identity. When we play our role based on ideas we get from others and we fail, it's not really our fault, because it wasn't really our way of doing things in the first place. Following others is not a bad plan. Except that being somebody else discredits our own unique history and experiences and leaves us unable to affect the world, or our families, with our authentic presence. The only thing any of us truly ever has is our own story. We might as well embrace it.

Although there are multiple examples throughout history of seemingly inferior or unqualified people being the catalysts for great change, facilitating world-changing inventions, or curing debilitating illnesses, my favorite example is from a movie. In *Legally Blonde*, Elle Woods, bombshell of a student attorney, wins a trial based on her cross-examination of the key witness, who claimed to be washing her hair at the time of the murder. Ms. Woods accurately points out that because the witness just admitted to getting a perm, she must therefore be lying, because freshly permed hair cannot be washed. A fact that opposing counsel did not know! All our experiences — no matter how trivial — matter. All versions of who we have been are relevant to who we are today. Our own unique experiences, our own stories, allow us to see things that others cannot, because they do not share our story.

Looking back at your personal evolutions and all that transpired to create the successful woman you are today, what are the stories surrounding each of these incarnations? How did the various iterations of self allow you to evolve into the fuller, richer version of who you are today, and how did they lead you away from your own center?

When we take on identities or personas that are not congruent with who we are inside or when we ignore evolutions of who we have been, we end up resentful, grouchy, and depressed. Adopting the lackluster, personality-free persona that I chose when I first went away to college ignored my identity as a perky pom-pom dancer, a perfect little princess, and a nerdy girl in glasses and did not honor my core self, my inner burlesque star, or my life history. As you know, my decision not to bring all aspects of myself forward did not end well!

When the way we portray ourselves on the outside is in alignment with how we see ourselves on the inside, we live congruently. Even when we take on roles that are not of our own choosing, by fulfilling those roles in a manner congruent with all that we are and all that we have been, we remain in alignment. It's entirely possible to do exactly what other people want us to do and still stay in alignment. It just requires awareness.

The Story of Our Incongruent Stories

I had two clients who each came to see me with the goal of losing one hundred pounds. Client A was my sad and angry client who had evolved into a loud, blustery woman on the outside but on the inside was tender and insecure and desperately wanted to get healthy and be accepted. She was a sexual-abuse survivor, at the hands of her father, and to avoid pain, she habitually covered herself. She admitted her sexual abuse to only a few, select people, and she bragged constantly about her life, making excuses for anything and everything that appeared to be less than perfect.

Client B was my happy, honest client, who habitually stayed connected to her core and to all evolutions of herself no matter how uncomfortable that might be. She exposed the truth of her life for all the world to see and incorporated all versions of who she had been and all that she was.

When I asked client A to do a food-and-exercise log, she presented me with a log that looked like it belonged to an elite athlete in peak training season. There were literally no suggestions I could offer her, because her log was picture-perfect. It was painfully obvious that the information she had given me was not accurate and was made up in an attempt to avoid judgment. When I tried to dig deeper, she cut me off, boasting about how much she knew about nutrition and fitness. She explained that her obesity wasn't her fault, that her body and metabolism were different from everybody else's.

She laughed when I suggested hypnotherapy to resolve her lingering sexual-abuse trauma, claiming that the past was in the past and that that incident was "such a distant memory," she was surprised she had even remembered it. Fifteen minutes into our first session she had already established that she could not be helped and that failure was not her fault. Her evolution had ceased.

Over the next few sessions, instead of doing anything I recommended, such as cutting down her portions, adding a daily thirty-minute walk, or drinking water instead of soda, she'd bring me copy after copy of miracle diets and exercise plans that she found online, telling me that she was doing those instead, because they were "much better" and "far more effective" than what I was recommending. After several months — with no changes to her body at all — she called and informed me that her husband, who loved her sexy curves, was upset by all the weight she was losing and she was canceling all further appointments.

Client B, on the other hand, brought a food-and-exercise log that showed room for improvement. She discussed the difficulty involved in changing her behavior, the struggle of having to feed teenage boys without eating the way they did, and the fact that she, as a former teen athlete herself, still felt entitled to eat gargantuan portions. She acknowledged the shame and self-judgment she felt in allowing herself to get heavy and out of shape, and was willing to get in touch with and resolve the hold that these emotions had on her.

She incorporated more salads into her diet, replaced soda with lemon water, and began taking daily walks around her neighborhood. Every time she fell off the wagon she'd laughingly reach out for another appointment and we'd get her fixed back up again. After two years, she had lost seventy-five pounds. But the last twenty-five would not budge.

Once again we did a food log, and this time, the item I

targeted was her nightly dessert. Sitting across from me, she folded her hands in her lap, sighed, and said, "The thing is, cooking beautiful desserts to eat before bed has been a part of my life since I was a little girl. I love baking, I love sharing desserts with my family, and I love eating my dessert right before bed. It reminds me of the time spent with my mom and my brothers, and it makes me happy. We connect over dessert, and I'm not willing to give it up. I'd rather keep these last twenty-five pounds than give up the joy of cooking and eating the things that I love."

In that beautiful, judgment-releasing moment, she came to terms with who she was, who she had been, what she liked, and how her body would look and feel as a result of her choices. Unlike client A, she reconciled all versions of who she was — internal, external, past, present, and future — creating a healthy, congruent version of herself that brought satisfaction on all levels.

Have you ever made up your mind that you were going to do something but then failed, despite the fact that you really wanted to succeed? Maybe you resolved to give up sweets but ate a doughnut at work the very next morning or a few days later. Maybe you decided you were going to quit working at your unfulfilling job or get out of your unfulfilling relationship and finally do something exciting and powerful with your life, but after a week your resolution for greatness fizzled out.

When we identify a pattern of behavior that we would like to change but are unable to do so, we feel like a failure. We may even be told that we don't have enough willpower or that we are weak. As a result, we fall into more self-judgment, and we feel guilty or full of shame about our failure. But in many cases, failure is not our fault. In many cases, it's simple math, and here's why.

The Conscious and Unconscious Mind

The part of the human mind that makes decisions and promotes action is divided into two different sections: the conscious mind and the unconscious or subconscious mind. The conscious portion of the mind is where thought, logic, and reasoning take place. It's the part of the mind where we make decisions, process, and analyze. It is this part of the brain that reads a map and figures out how to get from point A to point B. It's the part of the mind that makes logical decisions, and says things such as, *My knees hurt, my back hurts, and my clothes no longer fit. I'm going to lose weight and start working out so I can feel and look better.* It's also the portion of the mind that knows what kinds of foods and beverages are healthy, what a reasonable-size portion looks like, and what constitutes a safe and effective fitness program. Shockingly, this part of the brain represents only 5 to 12 percent of the mind's power!

The subconscious is the vast, nonlinear portion of the mind that makes up approximately 88 to 95 percent of its power and, therefore, drives most of our behaviors. Again, think of it as you would the operating system of a computer. We aren't typically aware that it's there, but without it, no other programs could function. The subconscious mind records everything that has ever happened to us, including our thoughts, feelings, and emotions.

It's the part of the brain where all habitual, automatic, and reflexive responses come from. The subconscious is the part of the brain that says, *I have delicious memories of being nurtured and fed as a child. Food means love, comfort, and reward! I've had a stressful day, and macaroni and cheese, chocolate cake, and fluffy rolls will bring me the comfort I crave!* And then, the subconscious floods the body with feelings of comfort, love, support, and joy upon our eating the exact foods that the tiny little conscious brain knows logically are not healthy and will not bring actual comfort.

See where I'm going with this? Everything we have ever been informs who we are today. We are emotional beings, wired to follow our feelings! It doesn't matter what decisions we make, how logical they are, or how much we really want to create change. What matters are the evolutions through which we have passed and what is contained in the subconscious operating system of the mind. When we make logical, reasonable, conscious decisions, we make them with only 5 to 12 percent of our mind's power, and we are not going to succeed. Unless the emotional, nonlogical part of our brain is also on board, our much stronger subconscious mind will win out every time. It's math. It's our personal histories. It's not willpower.

How We Learn

When we learn new skills, we do so in the conscious portion of our mind. Take driving, for example. Learning to drive means thinking about the movement of our foot to the gas, regulating how hard to step on the brake and how aggressively to turn the wheel in order to correct our drift, and assessing when we are close enough to a corner to turn on our signal. Once a new behavior or activity is mastered, performing that behavior becomes automatic, or subconscious, moving from the conscious portion of the brain to the subconscious portion of the brain. Once we've driven for a while, we drive on autopilot, flipping on our turn signal and regulating the pressure of our foot on the gas automatically, without conscious thought.

The conscious brain is small, and it fills up quickly. Because we need to stay fresh and alert, in case we are confronted with real danger, it is in the brain's best interest to move behavior down to the subconscious portion as quickly as possible. If we had to critically think about everything we did all day, we'd be too exhausted and worn-out to make it much past lunchtime! Think of how exhausting it is when we learn a new skill, language, or instrument and how, over time, when it becomes second nature, it is no longer taxing. This is why driving can feel relaxing, almost meditative. Once it becomes subconscious, it is!

Writing in cursive, folding laundry, typing, following the route we drive to the store, and brushing our teeth are all examples of activities and patterns that started out as conscious and became subconscious upon mastery. Once we learn how to type, we no longer consciously think about the movement and placement of our fingers; we just type! But here's the catch: we can't unlearn a subconscious activity using the conscious portion of the mind. As famed burlesque dancer Gypsy Rose Lee said, "Praying is like a rocking chair — it'll give you something to do, but it won't get you anywhere." Unless we engage the subconscious portion of the mind, using the conscious mind alone isn't going to get us anywhere. Read on, and I'll explain why.

Knowns and Unknowns

The mind is hardwired to function efficiently, like a computer. Instead of converting all information into 1s and 0s, our subconscious brains sort data as either *knowns*, if we have experienced or encountered them before, or *unknowns*, if we have not. All *knowns* are categorized by the brain as positives, and all *unknowns* are categorized as negatives. It has nothing to do with whether the event or situation is actually positive or negative; it's simply the brain saying, *Hey, I've done this before; I know this!* and sorting that piece of information into the *known*, "let's do this again" category.

This explains why people in abusive relationships repeatedly return to their abuser. Even though the abuse is negative and harmful, the brain categorizes the abuse as a *known*, which is always a safer choice than an *unknown*. If the victim was abused as a child or never knew a loving relationship, even though they may consciously desire a loving relationship, the subconscious brain categorizes loving relationships as *unknowns* and therefore as negatives.

Consciously we have the ability to think, learn, grow, analyze, and change behavior, but remember, conscious thought is only 5 to 12 percent of the brain's power. Couple that with the fact that subconsciously, new behavior is always seen as the *negative* choice because it's *unknown*, and it is clear to see that change is difficult to accomplish. No, it's not that we lack willpower! In reality, 88 to 95 percent of the time the mind tells us to make the safe, familiar choice based on old versions of who we've been. See why we have to take all versions of who we've been with us?

Creating New Habits

The first few times we choose something new, it is difficult, due to its unfamiliarity. But each time we repeat that new choice, it becomes familiar, known, and exponentially easier. Every time we make the same decision, neural pathways for that action are strengthened. The more times we make the same decision, the stronger that neural pathway becomes, and the more likely we are to make that same decision again in the future. Just like water running down a mountain, the brain flows to the deepest channels first, and until the smaller channels become established, it takes enormous effort to divert it away from the larger, established pathways. With each healthy choice we make, the groove in the brain deepens, eventually replacing our former default programming with new, positive programming.

Which is why the decisions and habits we create in adolescence and early adulthood significantly influence who we become later in life and how we can unintentionally get locked into patterns of either overconnecting to or disconnecting from certain aspects of self. Challenging ourselves by asking *Which version of myself is making this choice?* is enlightening and causes us to realize that even though we are grown women, with educations, prestige, and experience, there are still certain areas of our lives where our adolescent self, our child self, or a wounded version of our adult self may still be taking the reins.

Accessing the Full Mind

The conscious and the subconscious portions of the mind are divided by a filter. This filter develops between birth and about age six, and it keeps information sorted and stored in the proper location in our minds. The development of this filter explains why early on children are not able to distinguish between fantasy and reality; they literally do not have the brain development to do so. Until the filter is fully formed, the brain sees dreams, cartoons, and stories as all equally real!

In order to gain access to the subconscious portion of the brain, we need to open the filter. The most efficient way to do this is through hypnosis. Hypnosis is a natural state that all people move into and out of approximately seven times a day. We slip into a state of hypnosis whenever we become overloaded or stressed. Have you ever read something, only to realize that you had no idea what you just read? That was because you were in a state of hypnosis! The filter also opens up every night when we sleep, which is why our dreams can be such a crazy mix of fact and fiction and why we can sometimes react physically to something created in our minds. You know, like when you dream you slip and your entire body convulses?

Hypnosis in a clinical setting opens the filter and provides access to the subconscious portion of the brain, allowing us to rid ourselves of messages, thoughts, beliefs, and programming from former iterations of self that are not in line with the conscious desires of today. Hypnosis allows new, beneficial programming to be dropped into the subconscious mind, making it easier to create the new beliefs, behaviors, or attitudes by bringing 100 percent of our brains on board. Instead of struggling to overcome the 88 to 95 percent of the brain that is preventing change, we open the filter, align the subconscious mind with the conscious mind, and bring 100 percent of the brain on board. Which provides us with a much greater chance of success because we fully integrate our past, present, and future, leaving no parts behind.

Hypnosis in Action

Here's another client story that illustrates the power of the subconscious and the mind's propensity to choose known behavior over unknown behavior. Client C was yet another weight-loss client who came to see me because she could not seem to lose weight despite cleaning up her diet and exercising consistently for six months. We used hypnotherapy to explore her subconscious blocks to losing weight, discovering several subconscious scripts that sabotaged her efforts to do so. After that, we used hypnosis to rewire her subconscious beliefs to be more in line with her conscious beliefs.

When she was a child, although her mom and dad were good parents, their relationship was rocky. Shortly after the birth of her little brother, her parents divorced, and her family was torn apart. With the birth of the child and the stress of the divorce, her previously full-figured mother lost a significant amount of weight. Postdivorce she started dating, fixing her hair, and wearing makeup and attractive clothing, eventually marrying a man who, in my client's little-girl mind, took her mommy away.

That iteration of self tied her mother's weight loss and beautiful transformation to the end of her happy family. Although as an adult, she learned that her parents' marital problems began long before her brother's birth, her subconscious mind still equated weight loss and looking pretty with the end of a happy family. Subconsciously she believed that if she lost weight and started looking pretty again, her own marriage would fail and her family would be shattered.

Complicating things further, even though her own family was doing fine financially, as a stay-at-home mom, she was careful with what she spent. If she lost the amount of weight she desired, she would need to buy a new wardrobe. She did not feel justified in taking money away from her family and spending it on herself when she was not working. She was reacting from yet another iteration of self when she was in college and lost her work-study money, not from her current reality.

We used hypnosis to root out the subconscious beliefs that losing weight would destroy her family and take hard-earned money away from her children. We sorted through her unconscious, self-sabotaging behaviors and beliefs and, using a hypnotic anchor, provided her with a tool to help her choose actions that were in line with her desire to lose weight. Within weeks, she began to drop the pounds.

With this understanding, you have the opportunity to take everything you have uncovered about all versions of yourself and your past and use self-hypnosis to break free from subconscious blocks or programming that may have held you back from achieving your goals. The following self-hypnosis reprograms the subconscious mind; brings it into alignment with your conscious goals, dreams, and desires; and enables you to build your dreams, live your sparkle, and re-choreograph your life in the most authentic and simplest way possible.

· ● ● ● ·

Self-Hypnosis Road Map

Remember that meditation and hypnosis are two sides of the same coin. While they both access areas of the subconscious mind, meditation is a more free-flowing journey of discovery, and hypnosis is more of a structured, purposeful trip. So, in order to create a successful self-hypnosis journey, we need a clear, structured, purposeful road map! Hypnosis unites the subconscious mind with the desires of the conscious mind, making new habits or behaviors easier to adopt.

Since real life is a tad more complex than a burlesque routine or an afternoon in the thrift store, where we easily and instantaneously shed one outfit in favor of another, take your time in creating your hypnosis road map, and make sure it feels right for you. Choose something that you want but are having a hard time accomplishing. It can be concrete, such as the desire to *stand up for yourself at work*, or more elusive, such as the desire to *enjoy your family more*. Look back through the stories of your life, through your various versions of self, and see if you can identify where your programming originated by asking and answering a series of questions like the ones below:

- Does your passivity come from your family of origin or a teenage version of self where you pretended to be helpless and demure in order to get rescued or fawned upon?

- Is it a behavior picked up in adulthood after repeatedly being passed over for promotions?
- In regard to a lack of heart-centered connection
  during family time, has this always been a challenge for you?
- Did it evolve over the years as more and more elaborate family rituals and responsibilities bogged
  you down?

Sometimes we know exactly where our programming came
from, and other times we have no idea at all. While it can be
interesting to learn where your beliefs were first created, it is
not necessary to know every detail. It is necessary, however, to
know what behavior or subconscious programming you want
to release, and what behavior you want to adopt.

Begin by making a list of the subconscious programming
you want to release, in clear, direct statements, such as:

- I release my negative self-talk.
- I release my need to "do it all," to constantly seek
  approval from others.
- I no longer find myself criticizing or commenting
  on others.
- I release my belief that women should be submis-
  sive.
- I am no longer affected by the negativity of those
  around me.
- I release my addiction to smoking.

For each of those statements, write out what your ideal
new behavior looks like. These affirmative statements are the
suggestions that you will teach your subconscious mind during
the self-hypnosis session, so make them clear and positive, and
write them in the present tense, like this:

- Each and every time I feel the need to condemn or judge myself, I find myself being gentle and compassionate with myself instead.
- Each day, in unexpected ways, I receive and gratefully accept love and assistance from those around me. I find that I judge myself less and enjoy myself more.
- From this point forward, I enjoy other people's unique modes of doing things because I find that I learn from them in unexpected ways.
- I take steps to show the world that I am a powerful, visible, and worthy woman.
- I create vibrant joy within myself, no matter my circumstances.
- When I feel the craving for a cigarette, I take a walk, chew some gum, and think about my beautiful, healthy lungs.

Another way to do this is by relabeling yourself in a way that's authentic for you: "Although in the past I used humor as a defense, I am now secure and confident in myself, and this defense is no longer necessary." Or "I'm healthy, fit, and strong. Every day I crave activities and foods that are healthy for me and my body." You can even use a more analytical statement such as "New behaviors become easier and easier each time I choose them." Or "I develop new neural pathways that become stronger and stronger every day."

Choose statements that feel right for you, are written in your own voice, and clearly affirm what you wish to become. You want to be excited by your suggestions, not roll your eyes at them!

Next, pick three *anchors*, which are key statements to anchor new beliefs into your subconscious mind: a *physical* anchor, an *intellectual* anchor, and a *spiritual* anchor. These are touch points to use in your daily life whenever you are confronted with a situation where you tend to react subconsciously and engage in behavior that does not support your conscious goals and desires. These anchors help move you out of your old, subconscious programming and into the behavior that is congruent with who you are now.

The physical anchor is a movement that can easily be done anytime, anywhere. It can be twisting a ring, putting on hand lotion, twirling your hair, or taking a sip of water. The intellectual anchor is a word or a phrase that is repeated silently whenever your thoughts spiral toward reflexive or unconscious behavior. The word or phrase reminds both the conscious and the subconscious portions of the brain what you wish to accomplish, pulling your thoughts out of the subconscious realm and planting them firmly back in the conscious mind. The spiritual anchor is the act of taking a long, slow, deep breath, making the exhalation longer than the inhalation, and consciously relaxing. The English word *spirit* comes from the Latin *spiritus*, which means "breath." In most spiritual traditions, breath is seen as the way to connect the physical with the divine. Taking a breath oxygenates the body, releases tension, slows down the heart rate, and connects you back to your highest self.

· ● ● ● ·

Self-Hypnosis Script

Using your three anchors, your affirmative statements, and the statements of subconscious programming that you wish to release, pick one thing that you want to work on, and read through the following four-part self-hypnosis script. Go to a comfortable, quiet place where you will not be disturbed and think your way through the script, giving yourself adequate time to ponder and process. Enjoy the experience — hypnosis is meant to feel great. The experience should take approximately fifteen minutes. Don't worry about forgetting steps or doing it wrong! Each time, you will become more and more proficient, and your mind will remember exactly what it's meant to remember.

Conscious Relaxation and the Creation of a Safe, Magical Place

Take four long, slow, deep breaths. With the first breath, relax mentally. With the second, relax physically. With the third breath, relax emotionally. And with the fourth breath, relax spiritually. Starting from your toes and moving up to your head, consciously relax each part of your body.

Imagine, visualize, or pretend that you are in a beautiful, peaceful, serene location. This can be a real place you've been or somewhere you make up in your mind. Notice what it looks like. In your mind's eye, look around and observe the colors, textures, and details of everything you see in this beautiful, peaceful place. Notice more details, smaller details. The more you notice, the more there is to notice.

Smile, relax, and start to listen. Do you hear animals, water, the rustling of trees? Listen deeper, knowing that the more deeply you do, the more you will hear. Breathe in through your nose. Is there a smell? Do you smell flowers, earth, sea spray, or fresh-cut grass? Run your tongue over your teeth and around your mouth. Can you taste what you smell? Is this place salty, fresh, earthy, or sweet? How does this place feel to you? Is it soothing and grounding? Electric and energetic? Revel in the wonderful, magical feel of your special place.

Descending the Staircase of Your Mind

In your mind, walk around and explore this place further. As you do, you will notice a staircase descending. A beautiful, safe, and secure staircase, and as strange as it may seem, it feels totally natural for this staircase to be here.

If you have not already done so, walk up to the staircase and look down. Notice that there are ten steps. At the top, where you currently stand, you are exactly as you are today. But at the bottom of the staircase, see yourself as you wish to become.

The person you see at the bottom of the staircase no longer _____ [insert a habit or behavior you wish to release from the list you made on p. 85]. The version of you that you see at the bottom of the staircase _____ [insert a desired behavior from the list you made on p. 86]. You do not need to follow a certain formula. Simply follow your list, and one habit or behavior at a time, describe the thoughts, feelings, and actions of what it is you want to release, and what it is you want to create.

Walk down this staircase, down into your subconscious mind, and as you descend, allow yourself to become the person you see at the bottom of the staircase. Physically, mentally, emotionally, and spiritually. Ten, nine, eight, seven, six, five, four, three, two, one, and deep sleep.

Each time you think the words deep sleep, *the filter in your mind opens and you will enter a deep state of hypnosis. In this state of deep, hypnotic sleep, you are suggestible to positive, empowering messages that are in alignment with your highest good. You enter a state of rapid learning and personal growth, and your*

subconscious mind easily and efficiently releases its negative programming and realigns with your mind's conscious desires.

Anchoring

When you are fully in touch with how it feels to be exactly as you
wish to be, use your physical, intellectual, and spiritual anchors
to key in these new feelings. Breathe, silently repeat your word or
words to yourself, and do your physical movement.

These anchors are available to you anytime in your conscious,
waking life. Use them to bring yourself back to the way you feel
in this moment right now: confident, satisfied, excited, and oh-
so-proud of all you have accomplished! You have just created the
change that you desire in your mind; all that's left is to allow the
change to manifest.

Awakening

When you are ready, count yourself up, out of your subconscious
mind and out of a state of hypnosis. When you do, you will enter a
state of full, awakened consciousness, and the filter in your mind
will close and will remain closed to anything negative, whether
from yourself or others.

Zero, one, two, three, four, five! Eyes open, wide-awake, filter firmly closed, sealing out negativity and limiting beliefs and
sealing in positivity, growth, and fulfillment. You are now ready
for the rest of your day or night, feeling positive, supported, and
no longer affected by anything that in the past would have caused
you distress.

Use this self-hypnosis anytime you identify reflexive, habitual
behavior that you want to release or anytime you experience
difficulty creating new habits or sticking with new behaviors.

Work with one habit at a time, be patient and consistent, and remember that choosing new behaviors is only difficult at first; it becomes easier over time. Remember, too, that hypnosis is not a magic bullet. Nothing is. Hypnosis is simply a tool that provides therapeutic access to the subconscious portion of your mind. It helps tremendously, but you still have to choose to change!

You have moved through childhood, reconnected with play and the joys of your heart. You have revisited your adolescence, recognized where your beliefs may have come from, and released subconscious blocks. You are primed and ready to soar into adulthood! Shall we continue this dance?

 · ● ● ● ·

Adolescent Self-Reflection Stories

What are your coming-of-age stories? Do they reinforce any inaccurate beliefs, rules, or stereotypes about yourself or others? Do any of your stories illustrate how you rationalized, explained away, or came up with reasons why your black-and-white version of "the way things should be" didn't fit with the glittery, albeit more confusing, version of the way things *actually* were?

Take a few minutes and think about the evolutions through which you have passed. As you transitioned from childhood to adolescence and from adolescence to adulthood, what evolutions did you go through? What habits did you develop on your journey to womanhood, and how are they serving you now?

Living in the rapidly shifting platform of virtual reality meant that we could get so busy pretending to be something we weren't that we lost track of all that we were. Write your stories in your journal, and use the "Living in the Glitter" filter questions to see what they bring up for you. And using music, costumes, choreography, and characterization, don't forget to burlesque 'em when you're done!

. . . . . • • ● ● ● ● ● ● ● • • . . .

Adulting: "Responsible Adulthood" and the Power of Shedding the *Shoulds*

Ready or not, at some point we all leave our teen years behind and enter the adult world. And even though many of us had the illusion that reaching adulthood would mean we had achieved a sort of award-worthy final destination where we could live forevermore from a place of certainty and peace, knowing what to do and what to wear in every circumstance, this was probably not the case. Like a big fish in a small pond who is suddenly thrust into a vast ocean, we discovered that adulthood brought increased responsibility, the tendency to enmesh with our professional identity, and the never-ending duty to do everything responsible adults "should" do. And over time, we developed a tendency to do more and more for others and less and less for ourselves.

Tell me if this scenario sounds vaguely familiar. You do the laundry, buy insurance, balance your checkbook, visit your family on holidays, clean house, spruce up your white picket fence, and provide healthy homemade meals for your family because those are the kinds of things you know you are supposed to do. But instead of congratulating yourself for all that you accomplish, you beat yourself up for all that you *didn't* have the time or the energy to get done. I know you can't see me, but I'm raising my hand so high right now! If you're like most women I know, and I include myself in this category as well, this self-depreciation leads to feelings of self-judgment, shame, impostor syndrome, mommy guilt, and unworthiness. Even though we are doing really great things!

So what happens next? We hide. And we pretend. But we don't dare *show* or *tell* anyone what's really going on. And that's the problem.

While it is true there are an overwhelming number of things that need to get done, exposing ourselves and our lives as the imperfect messes they are frees us because we no longer have to pretend we are anything that we aren't. When we show ourselves honestly, we get out of our heads — and our endless to-do list — and drop into our hearts, our bodies, and the joy of our lives. Which, interestingly, frees us up to get *more* done, because we spend less time dancing around, making it look like we have it all under control, and more time actually *getting* things under control! It also frees us up to be able to re-choreograph our lives in a way that truly make us happy, satisfied, and comfortable.

The Making of Our Self-Worth

As women, we've been conditioned to measure ourselves against external standards, always trying harder and doing more. But in order to thrive, we cannot keep doing more, living up to standards that are not our own. Instead, we need to develop our own internal valuation system, where we meet our own expectations instead of the expectations of others. And when we do, confidence and joy flourish and we are enlivened both professionally and personally, because all facets of our identity align with who we are and how we show up in the world.

Of course difficult things happen. Life is filled with challenge and setbacks. But in choreographing our own lives and committing to our own path, we develop a knowingness of who we are, what we value, and what is important to us, which brings an inner peace that no amount of accolades from others can ever provide!

Since we can only imagine, manifest, or create within the framework of what we know, until we become aware of what lies beyond that framework, we have no means of getting there, and we remain stuck. Spending our lives meeting other people's ideas of how and who we should be is like living with blinders on. Until we rip off those blinders, our perceptions are limited, and unless something unprecedented happens that shifts our awareness, we can never be fully free to live and dance with our own kind of sparkle.

The Dream You Never Knew You Had

This awareness shift is exactly what happened to one of my mother's student teachers. Eliza was a kind, compassionate, and caring young woman who realized halfway through her student teaching that teaching was not for her. She loved kids but felt unfulfilled and exhausted by the day-to-day requirements of the job. This had been her dream, hadn't it? Nobody understood her hesitation, as she was seemingly so well suited for her chosen career. She was encouraged to forge ahead and was told that she'd "get used to" teaching and that everything would be fine. Her head knew that she was "supposed to" grow up, find a job, and move into life, but her heart kept telling her that something was wrong.

Against everyone's advice, she joined the Peace Corps. She released all her expectations, and without any intention of creating anything, she was sent to Africa. She fell in love with the culture, the land, the people, the smells, taste, and feel of Africa! And once she arrived, everything fell into place for her.

Her life in Africa had been right there, waiting for her all along; she just hadn't known it yet.

When she returned, she sought a job relating to Africa, volunteered at nonprofits, and worked with African refugees, but the longer she was in the United States, the more depressed she became.

Despite the fact that everyone in her world thought she was crazy, she trusted her truth, and bravely re-choreographed her life by moving back to Africa. Where she met the man of her dreams, fell in love, got married, and started a family. To this day, she lives and works in Africa, leading a life that she could have neither prepared for nor planned to manifest.

When we release old narratives, whether created by ourselves or by others, and uncover our own magnificence, we give ourselves the opportunity to live according to our own desires, and our path opens up. Where have you been driving ahead, doing everything you should be doing and neglecting that small voice inside, telling you that there's something more? What are your stories where you did everything you were supposed to do out of obligation, not out of joy? Perhaps you let yourself be defined by your husband, your children, your job title, or the size of your swimsuit. It's okay to be proud of all that, but know who you are underneath.

And when you do, you step into your Naked Self-Worth and open yourself up to possibilities you may never have seen coming.

Exposing What "Lies" (Pun Intended) Beneath Your Elaborate Costumes

Sometimes the accepted cultural norm is not the healthiest or even the most logical behavior. Gossiping, complaining, and embracing victim consciousness, while all socially acceptable behaviors, do nothing to shed light on the lessons and beliefs of our past or inform us of our current reality. Similar to the way taking medication to treat symptoms is considered normal but doing the work to eliminate the root cause is considered alternative, so too have we gotten used to wearing masks, constructing elaborate costumes around ourselves and our lives, instead of revealing who we are at our core. Hiding behind our elaborate costumes causes physical, mental, and emotional problems that affect us professionally and personally. Living a cover-up may be the normal, socially acceptable thing to do, but living a cover-up is living a *lie*, and lying has negative effects on our health.

Concealing our bodies, our brains, and our beliefs tells us and the world that something is wrong with us that *needs* to be covered. Over time, we internalize this *Something is wrong with who I am* message, and we start believing that our bodies, our minds, and our ways of thinking and viewing the world are wrong, and the spiral of self-judgment and covering up is set in motion.

Studies show that lying is stressful. When we lie, our bodies go into a state of fight or flight, meaning that our adrenals secrete adrenaline, norepinephrine, and cortisol. These chemicals contribute to insomnia, nervousness, and lowered immunity. They make us flighty, anxious, and unable to focus, and they exacerbate perfectionistic tendencies. Worse, stress hormones speed up the aging process because they inhibit collagen production and reduce our cells' ability to repair damage. I don't know about you, but at my age, I find that little bit of biology pretty motivating!

Society encourages us to lie about ourselves, cover up the truth of our bodies, and use them for others' gratification but not our own. Nursing babies in public is controversial, but boobs on TV or in a magazine are fine. I mean, who doesn't love the Victoria's Secret fashion show? That's what boobs are for, right? Dress codes, oftentimes beginning in elementary school, reinforce the idea that what girls wear directly influences how boys behave. It's the showing of the female body that is dangerous, wrong, or immoral, not males' thoughts or actions. Rape and sexual assaults are underreported, with victims often expressing concern about what they may have done to encourage that crime.

Ponder the impact of the phrases we use with girls that we don't use with boys: *What will people think? Be careful; that might give him the wrong idea! You're just a girl. Be nice or they won't like you. Don't be bossy! You don't want to look like a know-it-all. Slut. Whore. Bitch. Cunt. That's not ladylike! Why would they buy the cow if they can get the milk for free? The weaker sex. You would be so pretty if [you lost weight, cut your hair, wore more (or less) makeup, etc.]. Is it that time of the month?*

When we get caught up in the lies, when we capitulate and cover our bodies, minds, or spirits in order to succeed, we become part of the problem. Our compliance creates a tacit understanding among everyone around us that who we are is wrong. But we aren't. Is it any wonder we're stressed, sick, burned-out, and frustrated?

· ● ● ● ·

Adult Self-Reflection Stories

What are the stories of your adulthood? Once again, spend some time journaling about your adulthood, and the experiences that have informed your perception of yourself. Marriage, divorce, death, loss, children, pets, and even travel have a profound influence on our identity and our beliefs. What are the stories that affected you?

For the final time, go back to the filter questions in the "Living in the Glitter" exercise and challenge some of your long-standing assumptions. See what it is that lies beneath your elaborate costume. You. Your raw, vulnerable core self who is amazing on every level. Or, as I like to say, your inner burlesque star!

But you know what else lies beneath? Lies. The lies you tell yourself about what you need to do in order to survive in a world where, despite progress, women still struggle for equality. The lies that keep you afraid of being seen, afraid that you are not pretty enough, smart enough, strong enough, or capable enough. Afraid that you will not be accepted for who you are. Those are the lies we've been internalizing since we were old enough to formulate beliefs and feel the sting of shame or the insecurity of being different. *Lies*, that's what lies beneath. Are you ready to end this cover-up once and for all?

Come with me; through *FLAUNT!* I'll show you how!

ACT II

REVEAL

Responsibility for Someone ... Else
Their Else becomes me, not becoming for me, or to me,
But becomes me.
And I am no longer me. I have been invaded by an interloper
Who, once inside, inhabits my Beating Heart.
Beating it for them. As I struggle
To find, or remember, or reveal the rhythms of my own heart.
Of my own becoming.
Because, I came for them.

— LORA CHEADLE

Who did you come here for? Are you living in a way that stimulates your soul, satisfies your mind, and brings you unbridled joy; or are you living for someone else, managing your existence, with just enough happy moments to get you through?

When we get naked, remove our masks, our carefully constructed layers of protection, and face our deepest fears — of being judged, being dismissed, or not being worthy — we reveal to ourselves and to the world exactly who we are inside, at our deepest, most authentic core. Which may seem terrifying! After all, if we are already afraid of being fully seen, of being rejected for who we are, then why would we expose ourselves further and reveal the tenderest parts of ourselves for all the world to see?

Because, as crazy as it may seem, revealing ourselves fully sets us free in the most sacred and divine sense imaginable. It enables us to find a deep sense of meaning, connection, and joy in living that cannot be realized by those who remain covered. Oscar Wilde was right when he said, "To live is the rarest thing in the world. Most people exist, that is all."

Living takes both intention and the realization that, like it or not, we are the choreographers of our own lives. Unless we actively choreograph, it is being done *for* us. "Sitting one out" does not pause the music in the dance of life in the way we might think. The dance never stops, and unless we actively choose our next steps, somebody else will.

What do you choose? Are you going to step onto the dance floor and reveal yourself so you can live deeply and deliciously, or are you going to sit by the wall, hoping someone asks you to dance?

Stepping onto the Dance Floor and into Your Naked Self-Worth

Doing things that scare or intimidate us, but in a playful way, brings the realization that our fears are often bigger and scarier than the thing we are afraid of. Instead of fighting against our fears and inhibitions, petrified that others will see our fear of criticism, our shame at being judged, or our heart-stopping panic that we will never find love, we expose our fears and bring them into the light. Where they can be seen clearly, held with reverence and compassion, and reduced to their proper size.

While none of us alone has the power to change that which is outside us, we have absolute control over our response. When we reveal our inner burlesque star, we regain our power because we no longer live in fear that someone is going to find out something about us that we don't want them to know. We dare to fall in love with our beautiful, miraculous bodies *exactly as they are*, and we wear what we love with confidence. We wholeheartedly engage in activities that bring us joy without concern that we're too old or too inept. We say *yes* to living in big, bold ways but with comfort and ease instead of stress and concern.

When we unleash the full force of our intellect and beliefs, we stand calm and unapologetic in our truth. There's no longer the need to argue, defend ourselves, or swallow our words, because we have embraced our raw worthiness. Living without cover means living without toxic self-judgment, guilt, or shame but as we authentically are. We reclaim our authority, because instead of frantically trying to control others and their perception of us, we turn inward and choreograph our own dance.

When we respond to limiting beliefs about women by being wickedly smart, deeply spiritual, and sexy as hell, *all at the same time*, we can't help but invalidate and shift the beliefs of others as well, by instigating subtle change in our daily interactions. When we reveal ourselves, exactly as we are, and we openly love our bodies, our age, and everything about ourselves and our lives, we slowly strip away cultural beliefs that women must wear a certain size, look a certain way, or have a certain amount in their bank account in order to be worthy.

I'm not saying that revealing your inner burlesque star will be the catalyst that shifts the worldwide perception of women …but I'm not saying that it won't, either! After all, all revolutions start with a single spark(le)!

Your Naked Self-Worth

Naked Self-Worth is the ability to show, and embrace, all facets of who you are — whether emotional, intellectual, or physical — without cover, without seeking to please or conform, and to value yourself exactly as you are.

Have you noticed that it's one thing to learn something provocative and exciting, but it's another thing altogether to apply that enticing new material to your own life? That's how it worked for me when I began the process of stripping out of my judgments, inhibitions, and belief that I had to be the picture-perfect representation of what I thought I was supposed to be.

Although I was tired of overfunctioning and being underappreciated, I couldn't figure out *how* to put myself first and also take care of the multitude of things that legitimately needed taking care of. No matter how many books I read, seminars I attended, or experts I talked with, I really had no idea what I was doing.

Which led to impostor syndrome.

Which led to more toxic self-judgment and more covering.

Determined not to fail, I kept layering it on, adding more and more to my already crazy schedule, in hopes that the next thing would be *the* thing that would ensure success, create harmony, and bring peace and calm in my heart and home.

Have you noticed that in life, as opposed to in business or in school, there are no markers of success along the way? There are times it's really difficult to gauge how things are going! Which makes it hard to set something down and enjoy relaxation or self-care when it feels like everything might come crashing down around you if you do. Which, in the short run, before others step in, it might. But I also know that if you don't, something's going to give, and that something is your health, sanity, or most precious relationships. And those are the things that nobody can step in and save except you.

Ironically, for a perfectionist like me, it was making an error that spurred me into revealing myself and discovering my own Naked Self-Worth. And once I did, I was able to *FLAUNT!* and make myself the star of my own life. I joyfully flirted with my fetishes, and laughing out loud, I accepted *what is* unconditionally, unhooked my constricting underwire bra, and let it all hang out!

CHAPTER 4

Revealing My Sparkle through the
First Three Steps of FLAUNT!

*S*parkly bra in hand, dangling it teasingly out to my side, I paused and watched my shadow dance against the back wall of the stage before wrapping my feather fans around my waist and turning toward the crowd. The joy in my heart was so immense, my journey to this point so unexpected. How had I ever gone from being a corporate attorney to doing something like *this*? Something that I hadn't even known existed!

FLAUNT! Step 1: Finding My Fetish

One day, in my weekly boot-camp class, a woman mentioned that her daughter had taken a pole-dancing class. Everybody giggled and *Oh-my*ed, but the words *pole-dancing class* reminded me of the wild abandon that I felt as a little girl twirling on the bars at recess. I remembered the power and satisfaction I felt pushing myself to learn new tricks, and I suddenly longed to be that girl again, instead of *just Mom*, who always played it safe and knew exactly what to do. The women continued to giggle about pole dancing. I smiled and laughed, too, but it was only to keep from crying.

I don't think I'm unique in feeling nostalgic or being somewhat saddened by the letdown of adult life. We all have times when we put too many expectations on a single moment, and we end up disappointed. My life was pretty darned good. I had mastered my *suburban mom* role perfectly, and I thought that adequately fulfilling the roles of lawyer, wife, business owner, fitness instructor, and friend "should" be enough. But it wasn't. I had never considered *Lora* to be a role that also needed filling, so I lived my life feeling more like the manager *of* it than a participant *in* it.

Finishing class, I came home to tackle my backlog of emails. As I clicked away, a picture caught my eye. It was a tasteful-yet-somewhat-sexy picture of a woman about my age. It was an advertisement for a boudoir photo shoot done by a team of women. I had never heard of anything like this before! Curious and hoping to find out more, I clicked the "buy now" link. "Thank you for your order" popped up. My credit-card information had been stored from my last purchase! What an expensive and stupid error!

If you have ever made an impulse buy or spent way too much money and regretted it the next day, you know exactly how sick I felt. I had just spent ninety-nine dollars on something pointless and embarrassing. What was I ever going to do with a sexy picture of myself? And who was I kidding? I was not sexy! I called the studio in an attempt to cancel, and unable to do so, I decided to schedule the shoot quickly so I could put this whole ordeal behind me.

The day of my shoot, I packed the kids off to school, shoved some lingerie and heels in my gym bag, and traipsed through the snow in my sweats and boots to my appointment. Feeling stiff, awkward, and stupid, I allowed the photographer to help me pose, as she explained which angles were good for my body. Before long, we were laughing it up, and I was having a ton of fun! It felt good to do something so outside my comfort zone that was strictly for me.

Two weeks later, the day of reckoning arrived. It was time to go see the actual pictures, which I really didn't want to do. I knew that there was going to be a huge gap between the way I thought I looked and the way I actually looked, and I didn't want my fun memory of the day of the shoot to be destroyed by reality.

Arriving at the studio, I was ushered into a private viewing room with a plush couch and a flat-screen TV. They handed me a glass of sparkling lemon water and dimmed the lights, and on the screen in front of me appeared a gorgeous, artistic black-and-white photograph of a woman.

While I loved everything about the picture, I was disappointed that I couldn't just see my own photos and get back home. But something was so familiar about the photo that I looked again. The lingerie was strikingly similar to one of the outfits I had chosen, except mine wasn't that sheer because it had been a different color. Her shoes resembled mine, too, except…

The realization was staggering. The outfit was similar to mine because it *was* mine. Those were my shoes because it was *me* in the picture. Me. I was the beautiful woman, and I couldn't figure out how that could be.

Not only did I select a picture that I was happy with, but I bought the whole CD of images as well! The simple act of seeing myself in pictures, from a totally different perspective, made me realize how much I had dimmed my own sparkle and light in order to fit in and muscle my way through life. How could I have looked into mirrors every day and not seen my own inner beauty, my own soul's light? For some reason, those pictures reminded me of who I really am and empowered me to make myself a priority in my own life, to put myself back on my never-ending to-do list.

Which meant having the courage to purchase the three-pole-dancing-classes-for-the-price-of-one coupon that I happened upon shortly thereafter, and confidently driving out of the suburbs and to the urban-chic studio for my first class.

After parallel parking the minivan, I grabbed my dance bag and hopped out, just in time to spot a young and beautiful woman in booty shorts, carrying a pair of platform stripper shoes, slip into the studio. I don't know how seeing that might make you feel, but my heart sank. This was not what I had in mind at all. The urge to flee was so intense that I consciously rooted my feet to the ground to avoid running. Who did I think I was? Visions of Cougar Barbie danced in my head.

While I didn't want to subject myself to the embarrassment of being the "frumpy mom" in a pole class designed for the young, strong, and beautiful, I was painfully aware that if I left now, I might never have the courage to stretch myself again. I took a deep breath and walked toward the door.

There were women of all different ages and all different body types milling around and getting ready for class. Although many of them wore outfits that left their cellulite and muffin tops clearly visible, nobody acted self-conscious in the least. Except me. I was used to hiding my flaws, and here was a whole room full of women wearing short shorts and bra tops, accepting their bodies exactly as they were, while I stood awkwardly by in my hundred-dollar tummy-control yoga pants.

Class started, and I couldn't take my eyes off the instructor. You have probably heard the adage "Beauty is in the eye of the beholder." It's very true! Although I was initially shocked by how *un*perfect her body was, ten minutes in, I was utterly captivated by her confidence and lighthearted sex appeal, and I thought she was one of the most beautiful women I had ever seen.

In the fitness classes I take or teach, I am used to hearing about the things women don't like about their bodies, things they want to change. It was completely different in pole class. The women there were wild, beautiful, and free in their dancing. They weren't covering their flaws or waiting until they lost ten pounds before they wore what they wanted, and they were stunningly beautiful in their imperfection.

I saw how my desire to be perfect had sometimes limited me, keeping me from the enjoyment and happiness I craved. I was ready to let that go and to join these women in the wild, beautiful, and free dance they were sharing. My tribe was here. They had been here all along. I was the one who had left them in my quest for the next best thing. I closed my eyes in gratitude and let my soul dance my body.

This is how I *found* my fetish. I was finally home, and I was never going to leave again!

FLAUNT! Step 2: Laughing Out Loud

We called pole class our "weekly therapy," and indeed it was. I left each class wrung out physically from the exercise and emotionally from the laughter. Pole taught me that all women are strong and beautiful, restoring all I had lost about the sexy, spiritual feminine and the fierce power of female connection. I had suppressed my sexy and feminine spiritual nature long enough, and it was time to re-choreograph my life in a way that honored all the long-exiled pieces of me. I still wasn't sure what that meant exactly, but I knew that it involved dance. So I decided to experiment!

Have you ever had one of those tantrums in your closet where you try on — and then discard in disgust — pretty much everything that you own? Because no matter what you put on, it's not right, you look terrible, or you just don't have the perfect shoes to match? Although deep inside you might know you are being irrational, before long you have spun yourself up about how ugly, fat, stupid, and pathetic you are, and you don't ever want to leave the house. That pretty well sums up my attempt at figuring out how I was going to bring back my sexy, spiritual self.

After more failed attempts at finding my fetish than I'd care to admit, I signed up for a burlesque class, which I didn't know anything about, other than it fit nicely into my schedule. I was immediately captivated by the rich history of the art form. Did you know that Shakespeare's *A Midsummer Night's Dream* was actually considered a burlesque? I had no idea! In the vaudeville era, burlesque dancers poked fun at the upper class's puritanical views of morality and decency by showing off the body and acting flirtatiously. Burlesque wasn't about sex or stripping; it was about irony. And society's hang-up over sex and the female body can be hilarious, once you think about it. One had to be intelligent to use and understand that type of humor. Can you see why it was so enticing to me?

Happy to have found something that made me so happy, I signed up for a monthlong burlesque workshop that culminated with a student recital that required no nudity or seminudity at all. Thank God! That I could do! The month flew by, and suddenly it was time for the recital. To be clear, goofing around in a class, creating routines, and putting together my costume had been one thing, but an actual recital was another thing altogether!

This time I wasn't being hindered by my knee-jerk *Oh my*

gawd, I'm going to panic and quit reaction. It wasn't my body, either. I was pretty proud of my forty-four-year-old mom body. As a former dancer, I knew my routine was pretty darned good, too. What held me back, plain and simple, was the idea that I was supposed to invite guests to my recital. Which meant telling people what I was doing. *Admitting* that I was doing this. And for some reason, I felt like this was something I "shouldn't" want to do.

Because having a brain should be enough.

Because being a wife should be enough.

Because being a mom should be enough.

Because how dare I show my body?

Because how dare I actually *like* my body?

Because I should be satisfied with my life the way it is.

Because if I wanted to do something so weird, so taboo, and so out of the norm, then something *must* be wrong with me.

Because why would any woman choose to do this?

Out loud is how *I* chose to reveal myself. By inviting all my friends, who turned out enthusiastically in full force to *laugh* right along with me.

FLAUNT! Step 3: Accepting Unconditionally

Having once again stepped way out of my comfort zone by revealing myself in more ways than one, I desperately wanted to challenge myself again. So when a friend asked me if I wanted to attend an audition for a burlesque troupe with her, I did not hesitate. Never mind that she was young, single, and in great shape and had this amazing urban-hip lifestyle. I was on fire and I couldn't be stopped. Who cared if I drove a mini-van with dog slobber on the back windows? This audition was going to be mine! I was going to own it, I was going to dance again, I was…

Being totally unreasonable. I was a mom of two, and things were *not* as tight as they used to be. Nor had I really danced in, like, twenty-five years. I had a family. And a marriage. And I was working hard in my career as a female-empowerment coach. Who was I to even consider auditioning for anything? Let alone a burlesque troupe! I mean, really.

But my dance fantasies wouldn't go away. Feeling a little guilty and a lot embarrassed, and even though "mommy guilt" was kicking in for leaving my kids on a weekend, I decided to go. Although burlesque embraces all body sizes and shapes, I was clearly the oldest one at the audition, and I couldn't remember the choreography at all! And then, midway through looking like Dick Van Dyke in a comedy dance routine, it hit me. I was an adult, and I had a choice. I could either enjoy myself or make myself miserable. I might as well choose to have fun. So I did! With great aplomb!

Driving the minivan back to the burbs, I felt so… *proud* of myself and what I had just done. Once again I had stretched out of my comfort zone, gotten out of my own way, released judgment, and moved into my fear. I knew I hadn't made the audition, but that wasn't the point. The point was, I was no longer going to allow excuses and fear to dictate my life.

You might be intimately familiar with some of those excuses: I don't have enough time or energy. That money needs to go to my family, not me! I'm too old, too fat, too out of shape for that. When I lose five pounds I will. And the biggest one of all, I can't do that! What would people think?

Exhausted, yet satisfied, I did a quick email check before bed. An email from the audition was already waiting for me. My heart sank. Even though I truly didn't believe that I would make the cut, the thought of being dismissed so quickly stung. But wait! I *made* the troupe?

How was I going to manage *being* in a dance troupe? This

opened up a whole realm of other potential problems that I hadn't thought about before. And then there was the fact that I was going to be required to strip down to pasties! Could I even *do* that? There was so much to navigate, but I didn't care what it took! I was determined to make it work. And for some reason, it always did!

Always.

And the best part? The teary-eyed women who would approach me after each show, grab my hands, and thank me for being bold enough to dress up and show my body, to run around and dare to be beautiful. Show after show, woman after woman thanked me for having the courage to show my imperfect body with joy and told me how much seeing me onstage empowered them. Although I never would have anticipated it, it did make sense. In pole-dancing class, the act of showing my nonperfect body with abandon and joy released me from the pressure of having to look perfect. I just never realized that *my* dancing burlesque would do the same for others as well.

Burlesque was the culmination of everything that I had ever done or loved in my life. It encompassed all my fetishes: from dance, and the accompanying rhinestones and glitter, to theater, and sharing an energetic connection with a live audience onstage. It incorporated humor, intellect, and irony, and it even embraced my spiritual side, allowing me to heal myself and others (unwittingly) through confidently embracing my flaws. I had struck gold that I hadn't even known I was digging for!

This is the story of how *revealing* myself allowed me to step into my own Naked Self-Worth and taught me to *accept* myself *unconditionally.* Revealing myself as I was, not how I thought I should be, showed me that who I am is more than enough. And how once obtained, that knowledge could never be taken from me again.

CHAPTER 5

Reveal Your Sparkle through the First Three Steps of FLAUNT!

Without question, now is the greatest time in recorded history for women. We walk around with minicomputers in our pockets and purses; things like antibiotics, vaccinations, and advances in health and dental care make it so we can live comfortably, for much longer. Infant mortality rates have decreased, dying in childbirth is relatively rare, and birth control is pretty darned accessible and reliable. In most of the world, women are no longer the property of their husbands or fathers and are able to vote, purchase property, hold office, or receive an education. And as such, women are shining brighter, building their dreams, living their sparkle like never before. And as a result, we are all living relaxed, happy, and filled with an abundance of gratitude, right?

Wrong. Autoimmune disorders are at an all-time high, and things like burnout, impostor syndrome, and adrenal fatigue, which never used to be concerns, suddenly are. According to the American Bar Association, successful, competent women, who have spent thousands of dollars and many a year getting their education, leave the legal profession at disproportionately and alarmingly high rates. Wow, who would do that, and why? Let me give you a hint — it's not because we aren't trying hard enough! It's because we are trying *too* hard.

Because we have only recently attained our equality, we are still collectively operating under the belief that we have to prove ourselves, to do more, complain less, and mold ourselves into the existing structure of the corporate world. Sure, many men do more around the home or with the kids than in the past, but for the average woman, who might also be working full-time, the *mental load* of the home and family still falls to her, and she is the one judged when the carpet isn't vacuumed or the kids show up to school on a snowy day without a coat.

Remember the dancing-backwards-in-heels thing from the introduction? Because we want to dance, we costume ourselves in the masks of the sometimes stereotypically masculine version of our roles, contorting ourselves into a structure that is neither sustainable nor enjoyable. Covering our smart, sexy, and spiritual selves creates the subconscious belief that something is wrong with us the way we are — otherwise we wouldn't need to cover — which activates a mild state of fight or flight, caused by not wanting others to find out what we don't want them to know about us.

In order for us to be immune to judgment, self-sacrifice, and body shame, and to harness long-term personal and professional satisfaction, we need to give ourselves permission to reveal all facets of our identity in how we show up in the world, integrating ourselves into the lives we've worked so hard to create. We need to get naked, to cultivate a sense of Naked Self-Worth, ensuring that we will never be undone by criticism, failure, or muffin top again.

To be clear, when I talk about *getting naked*, I'm not talking about nudist colonies or being sleazy or vulgar. I'm talking about emotional nakedness, intellectual nakedness, and physical nakedness in the sense of refusing to squish yourself into constricting foundation garments that you detest in an attempt to make your physical self into something it isn't. I'm talking about letting go of the ridiculous notion that "women of a certain age" should or should not look a particular way. If it's ninety degrees and you want to wear shorts *but you have cellulite*, wear the shorts!

Most of us have an insatiable craving to be seen, known, and loved for exactly who we are, not for how well we meet other people's expectations. Imagine how your life might change if you gave others — and yourself — the opportunity to glimpse you naked so they could see, know, value, and love you for exactly who you are?

How might this unconditional authenticity allow you to build your dreams and live your *sparkle*?

"I'm Not Twelve Years Old — What Is *Sparkle*, Anyway?"

All our souls sparkle; it's just that they all sparkle differently, and sometimes we get confused, thinking that we need to be *just like* someone else or have to act a certain way because we have a certain job. Flaunting is realizing that our identities and our roles are not mutually exclusive, and sparkle is what happens when we strip out of our masks and live life a little more naked, a little more exposed.

Although you may be a little uncomfortable at the prospect of exposing yourself, emotionally or otherwise (hello, devastating rejection!), think about it like this: Whether it's a first date or a job interview, when we meet someone for the first time, we tend to mold ourselves into exactly what we think they want us to be. "Football? Yes! I love football and international trade regulations, too!" But over time, we reveal more and more about our true selves. Maybe that we like watching football on TV only and not in the stands during a snowstorm, or that although we are an expert at international trade regulations, sitting in an office for fourteen hours reading about them is not our idea of a great career. As relationships progress, we slowly get naked, remove one mask after another, and allow others to see us, know us, accept us, and love us for exactly who we are.

Stripped naked and reveling in our own unique sparkle means that we have nothing left to hide and nothing left to lose. And the freedom of living like this is empowering beyond belief.

Are you ready to try? Let's *FLAUNT!*

FLAUNT!

At first blush, the word *flaunt* may sound in-your-face and boastful, like burning your bra during an HR meeting or wearing stilettos and your 1980s Def Leppard T-shirt to back-to-school night. But as women who command a certain level of status and respect, who have careers, families, and thoughtful, well-planned lives, we are probably not going to do things like that. Not that there's anything wrong with bra burning or freeing the nipple if that's truthfully who you are; it's just that many of us wish to proceed with a touch more elegance and eloquence, but we're not exactly sure how. After all, marrying our passion for radical self-acceptance with our intellect, status, and phase of life can be tricky!

As we practice the art of *FLAUNT!*, we begin to recognize some of the thoughts, beliefs, and attitudes we hold as belonging to someone else. And when we do, we might choose to release them, allowing the thoughts, beliefs, and attitudes that lie beneath to be revealed. Or, if the beliefs of others have served us well, we may consciously decide to keep them, integrating them as metaphoric foundation garments in our own lives. In either event, the slow, methodical unearthing and examination of the reasons why we conceal and reveal what we do gives us the opportunity to consciously re-choreograph our lives in a way that is raw, authentic, and fully our own.

Have you ever had the experience of learning something new and fabulous that you totally bought into and had every intention of incorporating into your life, and yet, despite every intention to do things differently, you couldn't seem to work this newfound knowledge into your actual life? Like me, you might have spent a sleepless night or two (hundred) lying in bed, beating yourself up for losing your patience with your kids, the day after finishing the most profoundly moving book on the importance of patient parenting. Or for apologizing and walking away, instead of following through with your intention to ask for a raise. As a female-empowerment coach who has worked with hundreds of women, I can say with certainty that we are not alone, and I can also say with certainty that this is something we *can* overcome.

Through the practice of *FLAUNT!* we let go of self-judgment, move out of self-sacrificing behaviors and mindsets, and fall back in love with our bodies, no matter their size or age or what shape they are in. The practices of *FLAUNT!* encourage a slow, steady shifting of our attitudes, understanding, and beliefs around the dance we do in concealing and revealing all that we are. They allow us to integrate the most vital parts of ourselves back into the lives we've worked so hard to create, meaning that we can sustain, over the long haul, doing what we enjoy, personally and professionally, without disease, depression, or dissatisfaction getting in the way.

We can read books all day long on how to play the piano, but until we get our hands on the keys and spend time practicing, we will never actually learn to play. *FLAUNT!* is about learning to play.

Concealing Our Bodies, Brains & Beliefs

The proliferation of significantly edited photos in the media makes us think that we are fat, gray, dimpled, and wrinkled in all the wrong places. We are fed the message that we need SPANX, waist trainers, booty enhancers, fillers, Botox, or surgery, not because we might *want* to do something that could potentially make us feel better but because we need to look a certain way in order to be valued and accepted by others. Even the diet-and-fitness industry focuses more on how our bodies look than how they feel. No matter how cognizant we are that the images we see in the media are not real, we still judge ourselves against the airbrushed and digitally retouched images in magazines and movies or on TV, and subconsciously we think our bodies are wrong and need to be hidden.

And even more perversely, we don't just cover the bad stuff; we cover the good stuff, too. Sure, we cover our cellulite, belly fat, or stretch marks, because we know we aren't worthy unless we look a certain way, but if we show off a body that's too good, we're attention-seeking sluts who are superficial and dingy. It's not just clothing that we use to conceal or reveal our bodies. We use makeup, hairstyles, jewelry, handbags, cars, partners, children, homes, and a wide variety of other glorious accessories to cover ourselves in worth.

How many women do you know who are comfortable revealing their bodies? Are *you* comfortable in your own nakedness? Women are nineteen times more likely to have eating disorders than men. The average American woman spends a quarter of a million dollars on beauty products over her life-time. That's a lot of time, effort, and money spent on cover-ing our bodies. Might we all be happier stripping out of body shame for good and wearing whatever the heck feels good for us in every moment?

I can hear you saying, "Yeah, yeah, I get it with regard to covering my body — that's different, because I'm a profes-sional woman in a professional environment — but I can as-sure you, as a smart, successful, educated woman, I absolutely do not cover my brains!" Possibly not, but could it be true that some of us, in an attempt to establish equal footing with our male counterparts, have covered a certain amount of our fem-ininity or have adopted a more masculine way of showing up in the world?

For instance, have you ever consciously lowered the tone of your voice or chosen to be less smiley or friendly at work because you wanted people to take you seriously? Are you comfortable expressing exactly what you think, asserting the full depth of your expertise, or do you sometimes soft-pedal your stance because you don't want to be seen as an aggressive bitch, a shrew, or someone who has a chip on their shoulder? Have you ever bitten your tongue while someone mansplained something to you, knowing full well that if you were a man, you would not be spoken to so condescendingly? What about being cognizant of the way you dressed, perhaps making your-self look less attractive, because you were aware of the belief that a woman can't be both smart and sexy, or that sexy women only succeed because they sleep their way to the top? Could any of this be seen as covering the full breadth of your intelli-gence? I'm pretty confident that most of us would rather quit worrying about what we look or sound like and simply let our intellect run free.

Finally, there's the way we cover our beliefs. Women consume 70 percent of the self-help market. This means that we seek out more help, trying harder to *fix* ourselves, trying to alter who we are, yet statistically we feel worse about ourselves than men. In a professional environment, as well as on a personal level, society tends to value the traditionally masculine qualities of facts, figures, competition, and less emotion over the traditionally feminine qualities of intuition, connection, collaboration, and emotional intelligence. At work, we are far more likely to cover the feminine emotion of tears than the more masculine emotion of anger. Is it any wonder that women are twice as likely as men to take antianxiety medication?

Traditionally, women have not been socialized to ask for, or accept, help in a healthy manner. We strive to be strong and independent, sometimes going overboard and overfunctioning at work or at home, martyring ourselves and becoming resentful that nobody is noticing or helping. Our language speaks volumes about women and our covered beliefs. Take, for example, how working women often talk about their mommy guilt, but the phrase *daddy guilt* doesn't even exist. By contrast, when men stay home to take care of the children, they are *babysitting*, while it's commonplace and expected for women to take care of their children.

We already know that there's a gender bias out there. That's not news, and that's not what I'm addressing in this book. I'm addressing *our response* to the gender bias. The problem is not that we have a gender bias. The problem is what we do when we are confronted with this gender bias, and how we perpetuate it every time we cover ourselves up and lie about who we are. The gentle, consistent practices outlined in the five steps of *FLAUNT!* change this response, because the steps shift our mindset, attitudes, and beliefs and allow us to show up in a much more sustainable and authentic manner.

Whenever we cover our cellulite or our exhaustion, whenever we jump on the bandwagon and judge other women for staying home to raise their families or for going back to work and putting their children in daycare, we inadvertently strengthen the very rules and judgments we are attempting to release ourselves from. Whenever we seek external validation, whenever we try harder to do what is expected of us, or whenever we live out a stereotype in hopes of getting ahead, we only make the problem worse. Our complaisance adds more layers to the cover-up and perpetuates the belief that we are wrong for who we are, how we look, and what we believe. When we get more caught up in being who we "ought" to be, and seeking validation for that, we become part of the problem.

What I want for you, what I want for all of us, is a steadfast refusal to cover our bodies, our brains, or our beliefs. What I want, for you and all women, is to be able to stand naked and proud, as exactly who you are. *FLAUNT!* empowers you to stop lying, to stop covering up. To reveal your light, as well as your shadow, without apology. Because when you are naked, when nothing more can be stripped from you and you have nothing left to hide, there is nothing left to fear.

Imagine a world where you didn't have to worry about judgment, where you could fully embody all your own gifts without reservation. A world where the voice in your head that tells you that you're an impostor, a bad mom — that you aren't pretty enough, or thin enough, or smart enough — doesn't exist. A world where you are free to spend your time and energy being exactly who you are. I'm here to show you that that kind of world is already out there, but stepping into that world requires you to recognize all you are covering and bravely reveal all that is inside you, dying to be set free.

Are you ready? Step 1 is "Find Your Fetish"!

FLAUNT! Step 1: Find Your Fetish

When you hear the word *fetish*, what do you think? If you are like most people, you probably think of things like furry handcuffs, whips, and leather catsuits. You may be surprised to hear that the actual definition of *fetish* includes both an object believed to have magical powers and an object of irrational reverence or obsessive devotion. Like Dumbo and his feather or me with my purse-size hand sanitizer during flu season. Whether we admit it or not, everyone has fetishes. Many of us are superstitious, secretly believing that things or behaviors can protect us or bring us luck. Fess up now! You have been known to knock on wood, haven't you?

Many mainstream religious icons, such as a cross, fit the definition of fetish. For a lot of people, wearing a cross or burying the statuette of a saint is believed to bring protection or luck. A fetish is really nothing more than unwavering faith, coupled with positive thinking. Which is why finding, embracing, and burlesquing our fetishes is powerful and life changing. It gives us a sense of hope and control in a world that can sometimes be scary. Plus, it's really fun!

Remember that a burlesque is a parody, a work of art intended to poke fun at taboo and the status quo. Burlesque is the perfect medium for instigating change because it allows us to look at the serious and painful aspects of our lives or our world through an ironic or humorous lens.

Here's how it works. When we experience feelings of hopeless disconnection and loneliness, it's painful, dark, and heavy. Dwelling on our helplessness and despair doesn't help.

But finding our fetish and burlesquing our situation provides space to step back; gain perspective; inject some humor, levity, and light into our situation; and gain clarity and focus. Which makes us capable of honest forward motion that would have been impossible had we stayed stuck in the dark seriousness of our situation. Instead of hiding your fetishes, let's reveal 'em, burlesque 'em, and have some fun!

I'll go first. For years I wore the logo of my gym socks on my right arch. No matter how much of a hurry I was in, if I had my socks on the wrong feet, I'd take the time to change them. One day, as a mature adult, I decided that my sock hang-up was stupid and it was high time I let go of the idea that the placement of my socks determined the outcome of my day. That morning I wore my socks on the wrong feet, and that afternoon my grandfather passed away. Coincidence? I think not. There is honestly a part of my brain that feels like my socks killed my grandpa. Do you see why honoring our fetishes is of vital importance, especially when we have relatives we'd like to keep alive?

And despite my joke, do you see how it feels much better to temper a sad situation with some humor? Telling my sock story at the funeral and having us all smile, laugh, and share our own crazy, inexplicable fetishes and superstitions made a tough situation easier to bear for everyone. And I think my grandfather would have liked it, too.

Flirting with Fetishes

As strange as it might sound, when it comes to finding our fetishes and doing what makes us happy, many of us have no idea what we want. As self-sufficient adults, we are more than likely not used to having people ask us what we want, so we don't think much about it. And even when they do, we aren't used to tuning in, listening to our bodies, connecting to our hearts, and figuring out exactly what it is that would make life juicily delicious.

Which is where flirting comes in! We flirt and date in order to experiment, to sample different kinds of people, to see if we like them or want to spend more time with them. Flirting is about having fun in the moment, without commitment. It allows us to see what's there, to determine if we want a second date or if we'd rather swipe left — or whichever way we are supposed to swipe if we have zero interest in seeing creepy Romeo ever again.

Flirting with our fetishes is exactly the same thing. It's dabbling, exploring, and allowing ourselves the grace and the space to figure out what we like. Let me nudge you a bit, just to get the ball rolling. What were your childhood fetishes? Children often have an obsessive devotion to a favorite stuffed animal, blanket, or toy. These fetishes help children feel safe and secure when they go out into the big new world. For an adult, the world is a lot more serious. What is your security blanket? Many of us put our passions aside so we can hold down careers, raise families, keep the household running, and participate in a variety of other "important" activities, and we disconnect from the things that make us happy and secure. Can you imagine how flirting with your fetishes might be fun? How it just might nurture you, your relationships, or your career because of the expansion and spark it provides? I can!

As a kid I had a fetish for dance. I loved the music, the discipline, and the satisfaction of accomplishing difficult things. I loved the beautiful costumes, makeup, tiaras, glitter, feathers, and shoes. I loved the sisterhood and the support, as well as the competition. I loved the way I'd get so absorbed in dance that I'd have no idea how long I was at the studio or who else was around me. I remember walking outside after taking several classes in a row and being shocked that it was dark or had started snowing. I'd feel totally wrung out yet satisfied. At home I had an empty room with mirrors and a ballet barre. No matter how stressful my life got, I knew that a few hours of dancing in front of my mirrors would make it all manageable.

It didn't seem practical for me, as a responsible adult, to divert my hard-earned money away from my family in order to take dance classes or to spend time I should be dedicating to my career at a dance studio. My fetish was something that I no longer had time for, so I covered it up. But covering it up didn't make it go away. Inside I still craved the pure self-expression that dance and performing provided me.

When I finally began flirting with my fetishes, I tried a variety of dance and movement options. Zumba? *No.* Belly dance? *Um, perhaps, why don't I sign up for a second session?* I "dated around" plenty, having tons of fun along the way but never finding anything I wanted to commit to. Until I took my first pole-dance class. It was as if the heavens had opened up and a choir of angels flew down and sang right to me! I was pushed physically beyond anything I had done in years, I was expressing myself through movement, and I was suddenly surrounded by others who were just as passionate about dance as I was! I had found a whole tribe of former dancers who craved movement, glitter, tutus, and jewels. There was music, sweat, and camaraderie, and there was work to be done and moves to be mastered.

Most importantly, I had finally found my fetish, and I was doing what I loved! I was a part of something that spoke to my soul, and I wanted to sob with relief, it felt so good to be back. Finding my fetish renewed me at such a deep level that everything in my life, whether it was related to dance or not, began sparkling with joy. Why had it been so difficult for me to see that taking care of myself, which made me a happier, healthier person, also made me a better person for my family, friends, and coworkers?

How can you begin flirting with your fetishes? Right here, right now, make a list of activities you used to enjoy or always wished you could try. Anything you enjoyed as a child or you wish you could have learned as a child, you can enjoy or learn as an adult. Whether it's at a local rec center, a Meetup group, or online classes, literally hundreds of options are out there for adults of any age to learn music, dance, art, foreign languages, or any skill imaginable. What is it that you want to try? Of course, there is plenty you can do on your own, but don't underestimate the power of connecting with others who share your particular fetish.

Being connected to our tribe is a deeply gratifying experience, and finding our tribe brings a sense of peace that infiltrates our entire lives on a deep, soul level. Finding and cultivating my *FLAUNT!* Flock has made me whole in ways that I didn't know I was broken. No matter what we love, no matter what our fetish — if it's acting, singing, cheerleading, reading, knitting, or participating in service work — there is a community of others who have the same fetish, and being with them changes everything for the better.

· ● ● ● ·

Rewiring the Brain with the Worthiness Meditation

Now that you've made your list of things you used to love and things that you'd like to try, it's time to get your head — or more specifically, your subconscious — into the game! If you've spent any time at all living out self-sacrificing behaviors, believing it's your noble duty to martyr yourself for others, then there's a groove in your brain that's going to sabotage you at every turn. Good thing meditation and self-hypnosis can remedy this! Remember the meditation we did earlier? Once again, we are going to use this practice to restructure the subconscious mind. But this time, we are going to anchor in a feeling of worthiness, a feeling that we are special and deserving of doing things that we enjoy.

In order to do this, we must tune in to the feeling of being special, worthy, and supported. Can you remember a time when you felt this way? Perhaps a time when you believed in magic, whether it was fairy dust, wishing wells, a rabbit's foot, or lucky pennies? Connect back to that time and see if you can feel how the simple act of finding a penny affirmed that you were special. After all, you were singled out and the magic happened to *you*! Finding your fetish is about uncovering this feeling of worthiness or specialness and allowing your heart to sing.

If magic wasn't your thing, see if you can recall the feelings of anticipation and excitement right before a big holiday. As kids, many of us honestly thought that we might catch Santa Claus delivering our presents if we could only stay up late enough, or that we might see his sleigh fly across the sky. We didn't believe in the tooth fairy, the Easter Bunny, or Santa Claus because we were gullible children; we believed in them because we knew we deserved magic and wonder in our lives. We knew we were special, and losing teeth and growing new ones was a miracle worthy of being honored by quarters scattered under our pillows.

Once you have found this feeling of specialness, of being deserving or worthy, you are ready to meditate!

The Worthiness Meditation

Find a comfortable place to relax, where you won't be disturbed. Take a few breaths and allow yourself to settle in.

On your next in breath, think about breathing in worthiness. Exhale obligation.

Settle in some more.

Relax, breathe, and continue to tune in to all you can recall about feeling special, worthy, and deserving.

Exhale the notion that your worth comes from what you do. Or what you sacrifice. Or what you achieve. Or anything that is outside you at all. Let it all go, relax, and sit with yourself as you are. As a worthy, special, deserving person, regardless of any condition.

When you are ready, slowly introduce the mantra "Because I deserve it. Because it's fun. Because I deserve fun!"

Notice if anything comes up for you as you breathe your mantra in and out, letting it wash over you and allowing it to connect to the feelings you remember of being special, deserving, and important. Don't judge; just notice. And allow yourself to remember and to feel.

When you are feeling as good and as special and as worthy as you think you possibly can in this moment, touch the thumb and index finger of your left hand together, take a deep, conscious breath, and silently repeat your mantra:

"Because I deserve it. Because it's fun. Because I deserve fun!"

From this point forward, this touch, this breath, and this mantra are your anchor. They anchor in all the feelings of worthiness, specialness, and deservedness that you are experiencing now, in your everyday life.

You can use this anchor anytime, throughout the day or night, whenever you find that you have slipped back into your old, self-sacrificing habits. Anytime you find yourself looking for others to affirm what you now know is already special and valid within you.

And as you breathe, and as you feel the touch of your fingers, your mind will remember these feelings, this power, and your subconscious mind will release all thoughts, all feelings, that in the past have kept you locked in a pattern of self-sacrifice or un-worthiness.

Breathe, relax, and whenever you feel ready, slowly let your mind move back to the present. Take three or four deep breaths, feeling the oxygen move throughout your body, preparing you for your day or night. Open your eyes, and once again practice your anchor — your touch, your breath, and your mantra — this time in full, awakened consciousness.

• ● ● ● •

Re-choreographing Your Life with the Fetish Finder Worksheet

Now that you've created your anchor and shifted your mind-set, it's time to get practical and figure out where and how to find the time to flirt with these fetishes of yours.

You can download my Fetish Finder worksheet by going to loracheadle.com/freebies, or you can make one yourself by making a grid on a sheet of paper. Divide the page into eight columns and twenty-five rows. Leave the top-left box blank or draw an X through it. Then write the days of the week at the top of the remaining seven columns. In the column along the left side of the page, write in every hour of the day and night (midnight through 11 PM). You now have a rectangle for each hour of each day of the week.

Fill out this weekly plan sheet, not as a day planner to specifically track what's going on in any particular week but rather to track what an average week looks like for you. Write in everything you do in a typical week, from sleeping, eating, showering, preparing meals, and cleaning...to working, commuting, connecting with those you love, pursuing your hobbies, working out, or watching TV.

Next, you'll use colors to sort the time you spend into five categories: (1) *Activities of Daily Living*, (2) *Work*, (3) *Home*, (4) *Friends and Family*, and (5) *Fun*. Grab five highlighters, crayons, or colored pencils. Pick your favorite color and set it aside; you are saving that color to highlight the fifth category, *Fun*. Using a different color for each of the other four categories, shade in all the things in your weekly Fetish Finder worksheet that fall under each category, and see where you stand.

Now, using your favorite color, the one you set aside earlier, go through and shade in all the time you spend having fun, chasing your dreams, and flirting with your fetishes. Don't be stingy! Include everything you do that renews you and leaves you feeling fulfilled, quenched, and deeply satisfied. Highlight every moment of time when you allow yourself the sheer joy of pursuing something you love.

Some things might fall under two categories; going to church might constitute *Friends and Family* time but it may also be *Fun*, because attending church is what feeds you, nourishes your soul, and allows you to feel uplifted and happy. Look at everything you do throughout the week and determine how you feel doing those activities. Like many of us, you might not be that tuned in to your emotions, and this could end up being more difficult, or more insightful, than you may have realized. Note when you do things because you think it's the right thing to do, when you strive to avoid disappointing others, and when you choose activities that nurture you. Your worksheet might end up being a mishmash of colors, and that's fine. This is an emotional process, not an exact science!

Once this is complete, step back, look at your week as a whole, and see what you have uncovered about your schedule. The weekly Fetish Finder is a snapshot of your life. Your feelings around the activities you spend time on become the emotional tone of your life. What emotions have you been building? Naturally, there are weekly variations, but this worksheet is the building block of your life. If your Fetish Finder has very little of your favorite color, you may be building resentment, exhaustion, and burnout. Of course we all go through different stages. There are times when we literally have no time for ourselves, and there are other times when most everything we do is focused on ourselves. The point is to make yourself aware; to recognize what's happening in your life, day after day, week after week; and to practice knowing how to make appropriate changes.

If you're anything like the women I've worked with, this worksheet will inevitably show that you're spending an inordinate amount of time on the *Activities of Daily Living*. In our time-crunched culture, many of us must find creative ways to pursue our fetishes, feel good, and get out of our heads and reconnect with our bodies whenever we can. If this sounds like I may be referring to you, see if there's the possibility of allowing your *Activities of Daily Living* to nurture you in some way.

In reviewing my Fetish Finder worksheet, I realized that it took me thirty minutes in the morning to get ready for the day and thirty minutes in the evening to get ready for bed. That was seven hours a week of purely wasted time, and it irritated me beyond belief! Because there was no way around brushing and flossing my teeth, showering, and putting my contacts in every morning and taking them back out every evening, I challenged myself to find ways to make those times of day something to look forward to instead of something I merely tolerated.

I took an afternoon and went shopping. I looked and sniffed and sampled until I found products that I really liked. Products that made me excited to brush my teeth and shampoo my hair. I even found a contact case in a color that I liked and then glued rhinestones on it. Seriously. Small things, but they were enough to change the energy of my morning and evening routines from dread into enjoyment.

In the spirit of the Zen saying "Meditate for an hour every day, except when you are too busy, and in that case, meditate for two," I decided to give myself more time to get ready every morning and every evening. Instead of rushing, I consciously chose to slow down. I pampered myself; I massaged my face and hands, luxuriating in the smell and the feel of my new products. I tuned in to the pleasant feelings of brushing my hair, brushing it longer because it felt good, not just to get rid of the tangles. I breathed, I set my intention for the day, and I went through my gratitude list at night. I changed my morning and evening routines into spa-like self-care that I enjoyed, rather than hurrying through them like obligatory activities to complete each day. Yes, it added another (gasp!) seven hours to my already jam-packed week, but spending that extra time actually made me more productive, because I was happier, centered, and more focused.

Your mission, in learning the practice of finding your fetishes, is to boldly claim one thing in your life that's just for you, no matter how busy you are, and to enjoy it. It's like balancing an otherwise healthy diet, perhaps with a daily dose of red wine or dark chocolate.

Although it is vitally important for our health and well-being to eat right and have proper nutrition, remember that food and drink are also fun. If we never indulge in wine or chocolate, we are likely to reach a breaking point one day and scarf down an entire cake, washing it down with a bottle or two of wine. Yes, over the long haul, 90 percent of our diet needs to be nutritious and thoughtful, but it is also wise, not to mention enjoyable, to allow 10 percent to be fun.

Life truly is about balance, and uncovering and exploring our fetishes roughly 10 percent of the time is more than fun; it's a necessary ingredient for a happy and successful life!

· · · · · • • • ● ● ● ● ● • • • · · · ·

The Art of the Tease

Life, like burlesque, is all about the tease. The phrase *art of the tease* describes the balance of give and take in a routine, the timing of the reveal, and the creation of tension in order to build anticipation. Tension makes excitement mount and increases satisfaction, but too much leads to frustration, so balance is important. Finding our fetish and revealing our sparkle while excelling at life and maintaining relationships is the balance that we need to strike if we want the opportunity to enjoy this life we're living.

There's a part of me that loves setting and attaining goals, accomplishing whatever I set out to accomplish, giving of myself tirelessly, and making things happen. Which is why I love doing laundry. Maybe you enjoy that, too! To have a task and successfully bring that task to a conclusion is deeply satisfying. But so is executing tasks that have no tangible direction or results. And as overachievers sometimes forget, finding the right tension between our need to conquer the world and enjoying activities that have no concrete measures of success is what allows us to live a balanced, healthy, happy life; sustain ourselves; and flourish.

In a good burlesque routine, the balance of give and take

is what builds tension and leaves the audience enjoying themselves and wanting more. In fact, just about every art form uses this teasing between two polarities in order to create interest. Whether in music, painting, dance, or drama, if there is no conflict, there truly is no story! But it's not the creation of endless tension alone that maximizes excitement; it's the resolution of that tension that brings fulfillment. Is this sounding suspiciously like sex? I thought it might! A burlesque routine where the dancer repeats the same dance step over and over, never taking off her costume or revealing anything more about herself, is boring. So is a dancer who moves too fast, coming onstage and whipping off her clothes. In both instances, no tension has been created. There is no balance between polarities, and there is no joy or fulfillment.

What is the state of your life? Are you plodding along, repeating the same dance over and over, day after day, and never revealing more about yourself? How many years in a row have you made that same New Year's resolution? Goals are fine, attaining those goals is even better, but unless they are balanced with joyful, creative, directionless spaces, there is no tension. There is no polarity and no satisfaction. A life where we cook, clean, work, parent, partner, and exercise in endless cycles of "what I really should be doing next" is not a satisfying life. It's a hamster wheel. Are you allowing yourself time off the wheel to connect to the things you love, for no reason other than the fact that you love them?

Remember playing and our field trip to the toy store? Kids play for the sake of playing. They don't play in order to accomplish something. When was the last time you did anything for no reason other than that it was fun? I thought so. There needs to be tension between cleaning the house, putting the laundry away, successfully submitting your next proposal...and engaging in non-results-driven activities that nurture you. Putting yourself last isn't going to get you an award. Trust me, nobody notices your last-place status but you. Putting yourself last assures that you will always be behind. To connect with our lives, we need to place ourselves *in* our lives, not *behind* our lives, pushing for all we are worth.

· ● ● ● ·

What You Conceal, What You Reveal

Write down five to seven words that describe you. The deeper layer of you, not your job, what you do, or who you are in relation to other people but the real you, deep inside. Think back to the "Poppin' Tags" exercise in Act I, where we created two identities at the thrift store: our everyday persona and our all-powerful altar ego. The words you write down should describe your altar ego, the most powerful, authentic version of who you are. We are going to replace that base layer of childhood shame and indoctrination with undergarments fashioned from these words, so make sure they truly represent the most positive aspects of who you are at your deepest core.

For each word, ask yourself if you are proud of that aspect of self and like to reveal it, or if you are embarrassed by it and would rather keep it hidden. If one of your words was *passionate* and you are proud of being passionate, are you overly exposing that attribute? Remember the story of me in high school where I began wearing shorter and shorter skirts? Short skirts were authentically me. Microminis were an overexposure of a part of me that I tried too hard to show off. If you are known as a passionate litigator, wonderful! Own that passion, but be mindful of the fact that showing off can be an overexposure that creates no tension, provides no tease, and sucks the life out of an otherwise joyful experience.

If you are embarrassed by your trait, what is the root cause of that shame? Many women have been conditioned to meet everyone else's needs and deny their own. This mindset actually causes them to be embarrassed, believing that if they expose needs or desires of their own, they are selfish or unworthy. So they stay safely underexposed, with their needs and wants kept securely in check.

Could this be true for you? Are you a perfectionist, the one everyone relies on, the one who has it all together, and the one who takes care of everyone's needs, because you do it best? What a great way to stay underexposed, to stay safely disconnected from your own needs and desires! Sure, there's lots of tension in this scenario, but without allowing resolution in your favor once in a while, there is zero fulfillment! Remember, like a good burlesque performance, it's about give *and* take. You give. Now make sure you take.

Reconnecting with our fetishes does not make us selfish. It does not take us away from our families, our friends, or our careers. To the contrary, it enriches and enlivens us, providing us with endurance and enthusiasm to get back on the hamster wheel and do the things we "should" do. Which also end up being better, because we have teased out the fun, finding the right amount of tension and balance for us.

We have revealed the stories of our past, the stories that made us the women we are today. Let's continue to reveal the story of exactly who we are today, inside. Because when we do, we realize that we are freer than we thought, and we joyfully move into step 2, where we *laugh out loud.*

FLAUNT! Step 2 : Laugh Out Loud

Laughter shakes the body, causing the diaphragm to contract and release spasmodically, making it difficult to breathe and filling the eyes with tears. In moments of hysterical laughter, the head is either thrown back so the throat can open up or the body is hunched forward due to the force of the abdominals contracting. If you think that this description sounds quite a bit like crying, you are exactly right.

The physical action of the body when it's racked with sobs is pretty much the same as during uncontrollable laughter. Both laughter and tears provide a cathartic release for the physical body, differentiated only by the surrounding emotions. Although emotions aren't tangible, they are so real that they make the same physical action an expression of either grief or joy. This means that in moments of extreme tension or stress, when our physical bodies need some sort of release, we can summon either tears of frustration and sadness or joy and laughter. The choice is ours.

Laughter creates healing, boosts immune function, tones the belly, helps digestion, wards off depression, and may even help us live longer. But for me, the most stunning thing about laughter is its unique ability to ground us into the present moment, into our own lives and bodies. We literally cannot be in the throes of laughter and be thinking about our disdain for *that guy* from accounting or our disgust for the crazy black hair suddenly sprouting from our upper lip. Laughter moves us from our heads to our hearts, instantaneously. When we are laughing, we are all in. Period.

Think of how "nervous laughter" involuntarily erupts, cleansing the excess accumulation of stress energy, and helps our bodies feel more relaxed and our minds more in control. And because laughter is contagious, our ability to find humor in the everyday helps those we love feel better and stay connected in their lives, too. Women have been conditioned to avoid laughter and to refrain from smiling, like playing or exploring fetishes, so as not to appear weak. Have you avoided it in an attempt to be taken seriously, to not be seen as a giggly teenage girl or a ditzy blonde? Granted, it's not always appropriate to burst into hysterical, snorty fits of laughter, but it is essential to keep laughter in our lives if we want to keep *ourselves* in our lives.

I can recall many a tense situation both personally and professionally that was resolved by laughter, and I bet you can come up with similar recollections. Think of a time when something happened and everyone paused, not knowing what the reactions of those around them would be, but once somebody laughed, it was like the entire room exhaled. When situations tip toward laughter, problems are put in their proper perspective and the likelihood of universally favorable results drastically increases. Why would we *not* want that?

As a lawyer I was conditioned to be aggressive and advocate for the best interests of my clients. People came to me to have their legal problems solved, and typically those with legal problems, who are paying you by the hour to solve said legal problems, are not the happiest crew. Lives and significant dollars were at stake. Although I didn't realize what was happening at the time, in order to be perceived as competent and authoritative, I insulated myself from laughter, humor, and my innate, lighthearted grace. But the more serious and successful I became, the more stressful life became. Reacting to tension with aggression rather than laughter became habitual, as did my feelings of anger, stress, and burnout. And I had no idea why.

Maybe you're familiar with this or a similar drill: the one

where you shuffle kids from one evening activity to the next, struggling to fit in homework, baths, reading, dinner, and email, before tumbling exhausted into bed. Maybe you are better at seeing the humor and joy in the chaos than I was, but I often struggled against the flow, trying to be as competent and structured as I was at work, but to no avail. I could negotiate a million-dollar settlement, but I couldn't get two kids fed, bathed, homeworked, and in bed by nine? There was nothing funny about that!

One day, when picking up my kids at a friend's house after a playdate, I witnessed something remarkable. My friend, who had just as tight a schedule as I did, accidentally turned on the wrong burner of the stove. The wrong pan heated up, and as the taco meat sat there raw and cold, the tortilla pan with the pack of tortillas sitting on it got hot, melting the plastic package all over the tortillas and completely ruining dinner. My heart went out to her. I knew what this meant, how this one simple error could derail an entire evening, and I braced myself, waiting for her exasperation. To my surprise, she laughed! A full, connected belly laugh that caused her husband, who had run downstairs saying he smelled something terrible, to break into a huge grin as well. Scraping the whole mess into the trash can with a spatula, he said he'd get started on the sandwiches if she could bag up the meat for another day.

What had just happened? There was no self-flagellation, no tightened shoulders, no stress or irritation. The kids hadn't even noticed. Dinner was going to be on time, and the rest of the evening was presumably going to go exactly as planned. In my own house, I would have beat myself up with a "how could I have been so stupid and let that happen?" attitude, forging ahead with frustration that my kids were forced to have sandwiches instead of the balanced meal I had planned.

And the kicker was, I wasn't that person at all! I was a relaxed, happy, and playful woman who was able to see the humor in just about any situation. I was the perky one who broke the tension for other people. I was the sunshine-filled, positive thinker who could find a silver lining in any cloud. How could I have become so disconnected from who I was at my core?

I had equated being serious with being successful. I had worked hard to cultivate the persona of the stereotypical power woman, of a successful mother, but the personas I created were not always authentically me. As such, I often ended up with a headache, completely wiped out at the end of each day. Being my normal, natural positive self never made me feel sick or exhausted. I knew it was time to quit covering up and expose myself for who I was, not project who I thought I should be. And I knew that as a result, life was going to be a lot simpler and less stressed at my house!

Finding amusement or pleasure in things is second nature for most children. Simple games of hide-and-seek or go fish can bring as much pleasure as a day at the theme park. Kids don't judge fun based on how much it costs, how prestigious it sounds, or whether or not it's supposed to be fun. They simply allow the fun. Kids also don't see fun as something to be had after the work is complete or at the exclusion of something serious or more important that needs to be done. Are you like a healthily balanced kid, or are you more like the former version of me?

Could it be time to start laughing out loud?

Loving Laughter

Laughter is a base emotion that is part of every human's essence. But as mature adults, who have been trained that seriousness equates to intelligence and success, we can find it challenging to tap into our ability to laugh, let alone find and flaunt our humor appropriately. This is why we need burlesque!

Remember how burlesque is ironic, a parody, a travesty, and a glorious extravaganza intended to cause laughter in the way it mimics real life? Yeah, life really *is* a grand burlesque! And the next two challenges will help you see yourself and your life as the grand burlesque that it is, filled with irony, parody, extravaganza, and laughter. Like pouring water over the marbles in a mason jar, filling your life with laughter doesn't require you to give anything up or add anything more to your already overly full life. To the contrary, pouring laughter into our lives allows a certain juiciness to seep in and around everything we do, providing an instant connection between us, our hearts, and our lives.

· ● ● ● ·

Finding Your Burlesque Name

The first step in burlesquing your world is to find yourself a burlesque name. Pulling from your thrift-store altar-ego identity and your list of attributes from step 1, start playing around with names that suit your identity. You can search out names of characters in books, plays, movies, or songs. You can look at real-life historical figures you admire, or you can peruse the fantasy realm. You don't even have to be limited by *real* names! Your identity may be broader than a name that's already been invented. Feel free to adopt a color, sound, or made-up word as your identity. Burlesque is a parody. It's funny, exaggerated, and bold, so use your name to encapsulate all that you desire. This is not one of those stupid name-generator games.

Some of my favorite names are Ada Manzheart (say that one out loud if you don't get it), Margo Rita, Paul Bearer, Willy

Barrett, Ella Minnope, Anita Tool, Ray Gunn, Trudy Bauchery, Polly Esther, Deb au Nare, Cybil Unrest, Scarlet Letter, Fannie Spankings, Dee Flowered, and Bübes Radley.

My burlesque name is Chakra Tease, and I'm the Sexy, Flexy, Goddess of Zen. My name and tagline (no, you don't need a tagline unless you really want one) were born of everything that I love and hold dear about myself. The words that described me are *flirty*, *inquisitive*, *humanitarian*, *smart*, *spiritual*, *powerful*, and, of course, *sparkly*! Socrates is my favorite philosopher, and in law school we were taught using the Socratic method. As a yoga teacher and healer, I work with the chakras and the subtle energies of the body to bring peace. I love being bold and flirty, I am a natural tease, and since I've danced my entire life, I'm definitely flexible! My thrift-store altar ego looked something like Olivia Newton-John in the "Physical" video, a librarian, and a vintage glamour girl with wings.

My perfect-for-me name most certainly did not pop into my brain overnight. I mulled it over pretty intently for a couple of weeks before I sat down with a spiral notebook and a pen, wrote down words, jotted down phrases, and made lists of things that I liked or were meaningful to me. I pulled out some of my favorite books, songs, and stories, and I asked several of my closest friends if they had any ideas. I used an online synonym finder and got my husband involved in the process. Initially I decided that I was a *Flirt*, but I couldn't come up with a first or last name that went well or made sense with *Flirt*. One day I was shopping and I saw a perfume called Noir Tease. Until that moment it hadn't dawned on me that *Flirt* and *Tease* were synonymous! That night after yoga I was reading some philosophy and — *bam!* — the name Chakra Tease, sounding just like Socrates, popped into my brain and I knew that my perfect burlesque identity had been found.

Perhaps you are wondering, since *FLAUNT!* is all about removing our masks and revealing ourselves, why we need a burlesque name. We need it because most of us, despite being adults, still nose-dive into moments of insecurity, depression, or self-doubt. Our burlesque name is an anchor to the sparkly supergoddess or badass bitch who lives inside, who can do everything that we sometimes can't.

It's like this. As a lawyer, I had no problem picking up the phone or firing off an email on behalf of my clients. But sometimes I'd find myself sacrificing myself, downplaying my own rights, or putting up with things that I'd never expect another person to put up with. Whether it was negotiating a price for a car or an upgraded room when the hotel had made a mistake, there was a part of me that gave up more easily when fighting for myself than for others. I was strong enough to suck it up; I didn't need everything to go my way. Right? Wrong! Finding Chakra gave me permission to either advocate for her or use her to stand up for Lora's rights, which also allowed me to see the irony and humor in my situation. Kind of like how the cobbler's kids have no shoes.

So to answer your question, you are right! In a way, your burlesque identity is another mask. But since it's a mask of who you *are* at your most authentic, not a mask that obscures your truth, it becomes a tool, not a cover. Even the singer Beyoncé, as strong and successful as she is, has her own alter ego, which is essentially a burlesque name. When she needs that powerful reminder of who she is, she embodies Sasha Fierce, not Beyoncé. Whenever *you* need a reminder of your own divine power, you, too, can embody your burlesque persona and all your powerful, divine attributes will come flooding back to you.

Because as enlightened and as capable as we all are, there are still moments when we default into an incarnation of who we used to be: a scared little girl, an insecure teen, an over-whelmed new mother, or an unworthy, misunderstood woman. During those moments, when our confidence or self-worth is shaky, it is nice to have a fully authentic ready-made mask of us at our finest and most powerful core that we can whip out and put on. Think of it as your go-to outfit, like that one pair of stretchy black pants that look good in any situation and make you smile because they are so comfortable.

When you find your altar ego, your tribute to yourself, your divine goddess self, your burlesque identity, you recognize her deep in your core. Tap into her whenever you need a boost, bravery, or some badass bitchery. Like the most loyal of friends, she will always be there to make you smile with familiarity and joy!

Burlesquing Your World

Now that you have a burlesque identity, it's time to shift perspective and see your life as the grand burlesque that it is. The challenge of burlesquing your life and remembering to laugh out loud doesn't require any written work. It simply requires the dedication and willingness to keep your eyes open, your mind engaged, and your heart lifted and light.

Good humor, and burlesque in particular, requires intellect, so let's get academic about our humor for a moment! As the choreographer and screenwriter of your life, you are being charged with the task of turning your everyday reality into a burlesque. It doesn't matter if your current life is a drama or a tragedy; every genre is burlesque-able. Your challenge is to find the absurd in the drama, the irony in the tragedy, and to notice everything around you that resembles the extravaganza of a three-ring circus.

When things are particularly insane, I hear circus music playing in my head, and I see myself as the ringmaster, with everyone around me, the clowns running frantically about. Try this. I promise you will be a touch horrified by how accurate the comparison really is!

Let me share with you my favorite ironic thing about my circus-music trick for putting my crazy life back in its proper perspective. The circus theme song, the one that we all equate with 150 clowns in big red shoes pouring out of a tiny car, is called "Entrance of the Gladiators," and it was composed in 1897 as a serious military march honoring the Roman Republic! There's more. The composer's name was Julius Fučík. "Awww, Fučík!" Poor Mr. Fučík has probably rolled over in his grave so many times that he's bored a hole right through the bottom of his coffin. Tell me you love this story as much as I do!

Burlesquing our world and searching for humor, irony, and joy in everything is not about changing our personality or becoming a comedian. It's shifting our perspective to notice all the funny and ironic things all around us, all the time. What did you recognize about yourself and release in Act I? Do you tend to "be a grown-up," to stifle your own fun? Are you trying to be serious in order to be taken seriously? By whom? Or are you being stoic to prove your strength? To whom? Because I guarantee they aren't noticing. Do you hold the belief that life "should" be hard, and that you aren't doing life right if it is too much fun or if things come too easily? Can you see the irony and humor in that pattern of belief — how it's a *burlesque* for someone to try to be miserable in the midst of their wonderful life? Like mine, your life is probably pretty darned good. It's just that in our quest to check everything off our never-ending to-do lists, we sometimes forget to step back in and *live*.

As a female lawyer I was told that I should refrain from smiling so as not to appear weak, stupid, or flirty. Yes. And no. While I completely understand and advocate being appropriate — showing deference to, and respect and empathy for, others — gentle humor can be used appropriately, even in the darkest of times, to elevate and heal. Even if that humor is only in your own mind. Here's how you hone that skill. You practice.

Watch different kinds of funny movies and see what suits your fancy. Not everything will. Hang out with people who amuse you, listen to comedy radio, watch stand-up, or read books by people you find funny. The internet is a wealth of comedic memes and videos. Save or bookmark your favorites and pull them up whenever you are feeling low. No, you are not wasting time watching funny cat videos on social media. You are actually giving your brain a much-needed humor break, and you are connecting back into your own emotions!

Pretend you are a stand-up comic looking for material. Get a notebook and jot down everything that tickles your funny bone or strikes you as potentially humorous. Write down anything that could make a great skit. The best humor comes from real-life situations that we can all relate to. Watch the evening news and see what kind of *Saturday Night Live* sketch you could create from that material. Eye-rolling puns or preschool potty humor works, too. I don't care who you are or how many letters you have behind your name, it's totally okay to laugh at living in a place called Bikini Bottom. *Sponge Bob* is funny!

Life is not a battle to be fought or an agenda to be accomplished. It's a grand burlesque to be enjoyed. All you have to do is notice. Allow yourself to revel in your brand of humor, whatever that may be, and smile and laugh at things large and small.

Like meditation, a dose of laughter each day changes our reality. When we laugh out loud, we heal our own wounds and we fall in love with our lives by connecting to whatever is happening in the moment. Laughter moves us out of our heads and into our hearts and our bodies, so we can release all our head-based expectations about what life "should" or "should not" be like. Letting go of hang-ups, judgments, and expectations paves the way for the real game changer: unconditional acceptance.

FLAUNT! Step 3: Accept Unconditionally

To accept unconditionally means to accept everything as it is at face value, without letting our own judgments, expectations, labels, or stereotypes cloud what is truly there. As we uncovered in Act I, we are all products of our society and upbringing. Because of this, we all see things through our own filters, and we make people and things into what we think they should be instead of what they really are. And funnily enough, when they aren't what we think, we concoct elaborate stories, and we pretend that they are! This is the result of living in our heads, of not being connected to our hearts. And it makes us easily irritated by others and exasperated with ourselves.

The magic of accepting yourself unconditionally is that it instantly assures you that you are on the right path. Despite living a life you planned for, created, and really do like, have you ever spent some sleepless nights wondering, *Is this how life is supposed to be? Maybe I'm not even on the right path.* I know I have. But let me fill you in on a little secret. Yes, you are. How do I know? Because life is like a labyrinth, not a maze. There is no wrong path. There is only one path — yours. Being on the right path has nothing to do with not being on the wrong path. It has to do with knowing *where* you are at on your path, and the only way to do that is through your heart, not through your head.

If you ever walk a labyrinth, at times you may find yourself a little disoriented. One moment you will be walking along, enjoying the journey, and the next moment you will notice that the center goal, which you have been winding your way progressively closer to, is suddenly farther away! Or the path you are on veers off and passes right by the center. Or it turns sharply in the opposite direction, and away from the center you will go.

When the center is in sight and we are so close, walking away feels wrong! So what do we do? Well, we might stubbornly refuse to make the turn that appears to be taking us farther away from the center. We may stay exactly where we are, eyes on the prize but unable to reach it, because we refuse to turn around and momentarily walk away. Or we backtrack, sure that we missed a turn somewhere along the line and are now on the wrong path. Or we may plop down and quit in frustration.

Here's the trick. There is only one path, and that path leads to the center. Had we just kept going, we would have arrived at our destination! Even though the path is temporarily moving us away from the center, it is actually moving us closer to our goal. If we only had the fortitude to keep going when we were seemingly heading in the wrong direction, the path would have turned again, depositing us smack-dab in the center of our goal. The key to being on the *right* path is knowing how to assess correctly where we are along that path. To be able to determine if we are facing the wrong direction, frozen, or have turned around and are moving backward.

Accepting ourselves as we really are and not as we think we should be reveals both our divine destination, that which is truly at the center of the labyrinth of life, and our next step. Our heads may tell us one thing, but our hearts always know the truth. Accepting unconditionally means being strong enough to listen to that truth. Being fully grounded in *what is* makes us more effective at creating change than when we spin our wheels, trying to change something that's not what we make it out to be.

When we are able to get out of our heads, connect with our hearts, and *accept* wherever we are, *unconditionally*, we reach that golden AU level of peace and understanding within ourselves. (Get it? The chemical symbol for gold is Au, and we are on the AU step in *FLAUNT!* See, I told you I *really* had that periodic table of the elements from junior high memorized!)

Unconditionally Accepting What Is

At first blush, you might view acceptance as a passive or submissive act, but unconditional acceptance is a strong, decisive action that requires fortitude. After all, *accept* is a verb! To accept something requires us to actively take hold of what's being offered. It is not a passive resignation. Accepting is a choice we make, an attitude we adopt, or an emotion we feel.

Have you ever taken a yoga class? One of the things they talk about in yoga is the concept of *being* where you are. Which is brilliant, obvious, and really difficult all at the same time! In yoga — or anything, for that matter — we can only be where we are. If I want to do the yoga pose called *flying crow* but don't have the strength, balance, or flexibility, then I cannot be where I want to be. If I pretend that I'm further along than I am and force my body into more than it's ready to do, I deny it the opportunity to build the strength required. Who do I hurt? *Me.*

When we pretend we are further along than we are, we miss important steps along the way. Revealing our exact location gives us accurate feedback and enables us to receive proper direction. Think of using GPS without turning on the location setting. Without accurately taking into account our location, the guidance we receive isn't going to help much! Similarly, unless we accept unconditionally our own location on our life journey, the guidance we receive isn't going to help much, either.

We might know how to break things down, to do things that advance us to where we want to be. But when our metaphoric location tag is wrong, we spend a lot of time mucking around in our heads, instead of getting to where we want to be! The Universe responds from a place of truth and acts upon that truth in order to create the change we desire. Beginning from a point of fantasy blocks the Universe's ability to respond and create change, because doing so gives the Universe inaccurate information. When the affirmative thoughts, beliefs, and actions we construct with the conscious portion of our minds have nothing *real* attached to them, they just float around, and what we are working for cannot occur.

It's like this. If you are a student with bad eyesight and cannot see the board in class, and you refuse to accept the fact that you need glasses or contacts, everything else you try in order to remedy that situation will be useless. It doesn't matter if you pump yourself up, enthusiastically wanting to see, or if you squint, rally the teacher to cheer your vision on, advocate for better curriculum, or move schools. You are still not going to be able to see the board. Unconditionally accepting that you need glasses or contact lenses is the only thing that remedies the situation.

It's like forgiveness. Forgiving someone does not mean you condone their actions. Nor does it mean you were not affected by their behavior or that you suddenly forgot what happened.

It means letting yourself off the proverbial hook. It frees you because you are no longer involved in energetically *punishing them, showing them,* or *proving to them* that they were wrong. When you release yourself from them and their actions, you allow yourself to move on freely. It is not done by making a list of pros and cons or by thinking your way out of it. It's done with the heart. By connecting into compassion, understanding, and grace.

Forgiveness and accepting unconditionally are things you do for yourself, not for others. When you get out of your head and your beliefs about how far along the path you "should" be, and drop into your heart, you accept unconditionally where you are. Meaning you will know exactly what to do next.

The Golden Heart of Burlesque

You've found your fetish and you're laughing out loud, but are you ready to accept yourself and your life unconditionally? *Sure!* you might be thinking. *Once my kids get into college, I get my roots touched up, or I finish up that last certification, then I'll absolutely be ready to move on and to accept myself and my life unconditionally!* Tell me you caught the irony there!

Wherever you are at, put your hand on your heart, take a breath, and accept everything as it is right now. Not when something else happens but *now*. Get out of your head, quit focusing on what's wrong or what's lacking or what you wish were different, and feel what it feels like to be here, right now, with things exactly as they are.

No problem is cured by the same logic that created that problem in the first place. Whatever you've done in the past to create this dissatisfaction, disconnection, or need for something to be different, the same logic isn't going to help you now. If you want to change your situation, it's time for you to change your thinking. It's time to drop into your heart and your body and see what accepting unconditionally does for you and your level of peace, satisfaction, and joy. This next exercise puts you in touch with both your golden burlesque heart and the dark heart of your fears and neuroses, so you can embrace and balance both polarities and live a life free from embarrassment, hiding, or shame.

The Persona, the Shadow & the Self

Swiss psychiatrist Carl Jung identified several archetypes, or personality patterns, that all humans embody. Three of those are the *Persona* (the mask we present to society), the *Self* (our positive, conscious attributes), and the *Shadow* (our negative, dark, instinctual, or unconscious self). We've already dealt with the Persona and the various masks we have worn and presented to society, as well as to ourselves, over the course of our lifetime. Through play, costuming, and characterization, we have recognized and released these masks in order to reveal the Self and the Shadow hiding beneath.

Understanding and balancing the Self and the Shadow moves us into a state of unconditional acceptance, reconnects us to our hearts and our bodies, and ultimately brings us satisfaction with ourselves and our lives. Remember hypnosis and how our smaller, positive conscious mind could be derailed by our negative, unruly unconscious mind? Accepting unconditionally means cultivating an honest understanding of both so we can close the gap between the woman we want to be (our Self) and the woman who sometimes, quite irritatingly, shows up (our Shadow).

When we are able to balance all aspects of Self, Shadow, and our various Personas, we feel a deep, internal assurance that we are indeed on the right path, and we find ourselves more able to eke every last drop of enjoyment and satisfaction out of all that we do. In other words, moving into our hearts is like turning on our location setting. It reveals our exact location on the labyrinth that is life.

If you have ever watched burlesque, you know that it embraces performers of all ages, body types, shapes, genders, colors, sexual preferences, and abilities. Most human bodies do not look like those we see in magazines, on TV, or in the movies, and burlesque joyfully and audaciously acknowledges that. Burlesque celebrates the fact that however we look, we are all beautiful, sexy, and powerful. Beauty takes many forms, and burlesque flaunts them all! Which is why it might make you crumble, turning you into a mass of messy, grateful tears of relief.

While it's important to acknowledge and love our strengths, loving the positive attributes of Self is relatively easy. Exposing and accepting our Shadow in conjunction with our Self is where our true power lies and is what ultimately will set us free. Revealing our scoliosis-curved spines, unsightly scars, bags, wrinkles, gray hair, exhaustion, insecurities, vulnerabilities, and fears, and being so bold as to *love ourselves anyway*, is striking gold. That's what accepting unconditionally is all about!

• ● ● ● •

Letting Your Burlesque Self Lead the Way!

You have a burlesque name and identity. You've been to the thrift store and have made your body into a living vision board of powerful burlesque amazingness. Now it's time to claim that awesomeness intellectually, to own and accept unconditionally your inner burlesque star, your glorified, powerful alter ego, and all that she is capable of.

Begin by crafting a sentence or two to answer each of the following questions:

1. Who I am?

   My answer: I am Chakra Tease, the Sexy, Flexy, Goddess of Zen, a bold and daring sorceress who uses my gift of sparkle to empower women and bring joy to the world!

2. What is my superpower?

   Your superpower can come from your own strengths, from powers that you rely on every day, or from hidden strengths that you have yet to fully claim. Typically our superpower is one that we admire in others but we hold back from in ourselves. If I had a magic wand and could grant you any superpower in the world, what would it be? Your burlesque identity can handle this power even if you fear that your everyday persona cannot.

   My answer: *I am fearless.* And when fear creeps in, I rely on Chakra, letting her take the lead. She can handle anything that's thrown at her with grace, dignity, unflinching honesty, and humor.

3. What does my heart want?

   In three seconds or less, what is it that you want? Your heart knows, so don't let your head get in the way! Nobody's asking you to leave your job or walk out on your marriage. Just have the courage to hear and accept what your heart is saying. In Act I, where you wrote down the first stories that came to mind about your childhood experiences, that was your heart talking. The key in accepting unconditionally is acknowledging the intuitive wisdom of the heart and not overriding that with the wisdom of the head. Most of us have spent far too long chasing our heads instead of following our hearts. Don't give me the proper answer; give me *your* answer. What does your heart want? In two to three seconds, you should know. Beyond that, you are in your head.

My answer: I want uninhibited joy; deep, meaningful connections; and the ability to explore all that this world has to offer.

· · · · • • • ● ● ● ● ● • • • · · ·

Finding Your Shadow/Dark Attributes

We all have things that we don't like about ourselves. Whether it's our saddlebags, our noses, our teeth, some aspect of our personality, or our weird hang-ups or habits, there are parts of ourselves that we aren't thrilled with. Parts that we'd rather cover, hide, or ignore. Paradoxically, the key to successfully managing and diminishing our Shadow is the way we reveal it, not in how we conceal it.

Let's start by diving right in and acknowledging some of your Shadow aspects. What are five to seven things that you wish to conceal about yourself, your body, your habits, or your beliefs? We all get triggered and reactive at times. I have this terrible tendency to overexplain myself when I say no, regardless of the situation. What are some of your knee-jerk reactions or tendencies when you are tired, scared, threatened, and insecure or feel like you are under attack? Which body parts do you like the least? What about your personality do you try to hide?

Ponder this two-part question: *What are the things I typically do to protect myself, and are these really necessary?* Most of us have a litany of protective habits that we have employed since childhood to help us feel safe. Whether it's telling a little white lie (or a big, hairy black lie), justifying ourselves, blaming others, wallowing in shame and self-pity, or slipping quietly into avoidance, we tend to use the same tools, over and over, despite the fact that those tools are sorely outdated or ineffective. Isn't it time to take a fresh look at your stale habits, update your skill set, and turn your shadowy attributes into your greatest strengths?

Revealing and accepting your Shadow unconditionally gives you accurate placement on the labyrinth of your own life. Why? Because what we resist persists, what we are afraid of gets bigger, and the more we try to cover or hide something, the more it obscures our true nature, the center point on the labyrinth. Unless we bring our Shadow out into the light, it remains dark forever.

When I was learning how to stand-up paddleboard, the first thing the instructor did was make us fall. Intentionally! Once we got the fear of falling out of the way, we could relax enough to learn. When our entire focus was on avoiding the fall, we were in a state of contraction, restriction, and fear. Falling pushed us straight into our fear, and we realized that our fear of falling was more distressing than the actual fall.

The exercises in *FLAUNT!* are designed to push you over and make you fall, to expose aspects of yourself that you may not be comfortable exposing. Why? Not to be mean but in order to move you into your fear so you, too, can realize that your fear of falling is worse than the fall itself.

Embodying Light & Shadow

The Egyptian goddess Sekhmet is a perfect example of how to embody and accept your Self and your Shadow with balance, grace, and awareness. Sekhmet is known as both a warrior goddess and the goddess of healing, two seemingly contradictory attributes that, when integrated cohesively together, actually make perfect, complementary sense.

As a warrior goddess, Sekhmet, although powerfully destructive, uses her powers of destruction as a force for good. She fiercely destroys all that is evil in a terrible yet beautiful way that clears the path for good and allows true healing to take place in a way that could never be done without the clearing away her destruction caused. Her destructive, warriorlike nature is her Shadow, and it lies in perfect companionship with her beautiful, healing Self, making her gifts stronger and more powerful than if her dark side were denied. How could revealing and accepting your Self and Shadow work for you?

I'll tell you how it worked for me one glorious spring day. Perhaps you can guess, but I'm kind of a tree-hugging pacifist who would normally never hurt a fly. It was a Saturday, and we were at a soccer match for my older son. My younger son needed to go to the bathroom, which meant traipsing around the soccer field to get to the porta-potty on the other side. He wasn't little, so there was no need to go with him, but being a mom, I still kept my eye on him.

Chatting with other parents, I didn't see him exit the bathroom, but I did see a man sort of struggle with the door before slipping stealthily into the porta-potty.

I am not kidding when I tell you that something involuntary triggered in my brain. The next thing I remember, I was springing across the soccer field, through the kids, midgame, preparing to tackle and take down the entire porta-potty. From off in the distance I heard the parents I had been chatting with yelling after me, "Stop, Lora! Your son's over here!"

Healer, warrior. Let's just say I can absolutely relate!

Titillating Taboos

"'Titillating Taboos'! [*eye roll*] Are you kidding me?" Do you feel like a naughty, giggly preteen just saying it? Or do you disgustedly want to skim through to the next section? Either way, you might be a tad bit uncomfortable with where a section called "Titillating Taboos" may be going. Am I right? This is an example of how we get a little nervous (or maybe excited) around taboo subjects and moving outside our comfort zone.

Whether cultural, religious, or personal, taboos are thoughts, beliefs, or actions that we have been told we must shy away from, fear, or refuse to acknowledge. They reflect the collective Shadow and are important to explore, because even when they are not a part of our own individual Shadow, being a part of the whole affects each individual piece.

Regardless of your feelings about your own body, from a cultural standpoint, women's bodies, and the way they function, are taboo. The prevailing external belief is that women's bodies are there for men or children but not for themselves. Even strictly female activities such as menstruation, childbirth, nursing, and menopause have been taken over and made taboo by a male-dominated medical profession. Let's not even start in with sex and the variety of misinformation about the ways women's bodies work.

Wait a minute! Let's go there after all! Did you know that in most sex-ed classes the word *clitoris* is not even mentioned? Nor is female orgasm. This teaches girls that their bodies are functional, baby-making machines. That their pleasure, and the only organ in the world whose *sole purpose* is to provide pleasure, does not merit *mention*, let alone discussion! And what does this "oversight" teach boys? That male bodies are normal and female bodies are weird, complicated, and have elusive, unmentionable parts and functions that aren't even important enough to reference, much less understand.

Burlesque tackles these cultural taboos, provides the opportunity to act them out in grand style, makes fun of the inaccuracies on which they are based, and tests the waters to see how it feels to get close to them without fear of repercussion. What's taboo for you? How can you make a burlesque out of those taboos and bring balance and light to all that is dark in and around you?

Are you thinking, *Yes, Lora, I get it, but oh my gawd, seriously? I do not need to act out my taboos in order to heal them.* If you are thinking this, that is exactly the point, and exactly why you do! It's normal to feel a wide range of emotions at the thought of moving into your taboos, and during this exercise, panic, hatred, excitement, pride, nervousness, fear, joy, and exhaustion are all common. Your rising emotional current shows just how much energy has been expended over the years stuffing down and covering up your true thoughts, feelings, and beliefs.

Getting in touch with our collective Shadow allows it to emerge so we can recognize it, embrace it, and bring it into the light for all to see. Taboo is our Shadow. Accept and integrate that Shadow so it can empower you!

$$\cdot \quad \bullet \quad \bullet \quad \bullet \quad \cdot$$

Your Golden (AU) Statement of Divine Empowerment

Once you have faced your individual Shadow and mucked around in the collective taboo for a bit, the next step is making that Shadow fully a part of who you are. Facing your discomfort, challenging yourself as to *why* you feel discomfort, *owning* the answer, and transcending that which holds you back by writing your Statement of Divine Empowerment.

A Statement of Divine Empowerment encapsulates both your Self and your Shadow and, in language similar to that used in Emotional Freedom Technique (*Even though I* _____ [insert negative thought, belief, or feeling], *I still unconditionally love and accept myself*), allows you to succeed, thrive, and be happy, despite the fact that you have challenges and limitations. Your statement may look something like this:

I am modest **because** I was raised to believe a woman who shows her body is a slut whom no man will want, and she'll spend her life childless and alone. **This belief was bolstered when** the first man I opened up to left me. **I felt** violated, devastated, and betrayed, like he stole something from me, **and as a result I** disconnected from myself, blaming the failure of the relationship on my ugly body, my dirty sexual urges, and my impure nature. **Today, I confront my fears** and **acknowledge and accept my Shadow, as well as the cultural taboo and shame around** a woman who shows her body and enjoys her sexuality with or without a man, **by choosing to give freely what I fear will be taken from me. From this point forward I** buy and wear clothing that I like, without regard to my cellulite or my supposed virtue. I honor my tenderness, my fear of being alone, and I give my heart freely to those I enjoy for the sake of my own enjoyment. I nourish my own wants, needs, and desires without judging them but rather by indulging them, as I would indulge them in another. **I affirm that all I give fully and freely to others can never be taken from me again.**

Or:

I am uncomfortable when I feel judged by others, **which may be the result of** the way my dad picked on me, blaming me for his career failures, and my struggle to fit in with my peers. **It makes me feel** angry, defensive, and unworthy to take up space. **Today I challenge myself to move into this discomfort** by asking someone I love and trust for one piece of constructive criticism, and **I am going to practice breathing and receiving that which in the past would have made me uncomfortable,** understanding that feedback is strictly another person's interpretation of a situation that I may or may not learn from but which does not affect me or my self-worth.

There is no specific formula; it is simply a flow of recognize, release, reveal, and re-choreograph:

- Acknowledge the Shadow (*recognize*).
- State a possible cause (*recognize the root*).
- Admit your feelings and unhealthy actions around this Shadow (*reveal*).
- Describe how your Self will use this information to move forward and make proactive choices to dismantle or healthily integrate the Shadow (*re-choreograph*).

One of my clients, who was raised in a strict, fundamentalist church, wrote the following Statement of Divine Empowerment, which perfectly expressed her truth, embodied both the Self and the Shadow, and gave her permission to stand by and own her decisions for all the right reasons, without following a specific formula at all:

I know I'm not a sinner because I had a child out of wedlock. I love my child, and I loved the relationship that created this child. I do not feel like premarital sex should be a sin, but the belief that it is, is ingrained in me. I have a hard time figuring it all out. When I'm not going to church, it feels really hard. I don't like working so hard to figure life out on my own. I'm afraid that I'll turn wild and be a slut if I don't have rules that I "have to" follow. I realize that I like being told what to do by the church! I choose to remain bound by a church because I feel comfortable and safe, and I know I'm being the better person I'm being called to be. I'm not trapped. I choose to keep myself constrained by these rules.

This is exactly what a Statement of Divine Empowerment is all about! Now go and write yours.

· ● ● ● ·

Creating Your Burlesque Goddess Archetype Card

Have you ever played around with or seen oracle cards? Typically, these cards have a picture on one side and a brief description on the back. You are going to make a Burlesque Goddess Archetype Card, similar to the oracle cards that are on the market, that describes your inner burlesque star! Your card will have a picture of your burlesque self, a description of your positive Self and your negative Shadow, and your Statement of Divine Empowerment. That way, no matter how disconnected or out of touch you get, you can look back at your card and remember exactly where your power lies.

It doesn't matter if you use an index card, poster board, scrapbooking paper, or simply a sheet of paper. This creation is yours to do with as you please. You can use the picture you took of yourself in the dressing room at the thrift store or a snapshot of yourself that you have always loved, or you can do what I did and invest in a professional photography session! If you are the artistic type, you can draw, paint, or cut out a picture of how you see yourself.

On the front side, write your burlesque name but in a way that is special to her character and energy. In gold calligraphy, with bold red marker, using leopard-print stickers, or in some way that personifies the power of the qualities she carries inside. Think of it as personal branding!

On the back, list both your positive aspects of Self and your negative Shadow attributes, in a way that balances them fairly equally. Then write your Statement of Divine Empowerment.

Decorating your card is important because it moves you out of the analytical and into the creative. It doesn't matter if you use stickers, cutouts, or rhinestones or if you draw, paint, stitch, or otherwise craft. Just do something creative that is fun for you. Remember playing? Decorating your card is fifteen minutes of dedicated playtime. Enjoy it! Your burlesque oracle card is a tangible reminder of your inner world and your inner strength, so be sure to include any additional information about yourself that you want to reference.

This is your burlesque identity, your goddess self, and she is here to remind you of who you really are, whenever you are in a difficult situation or forget that you are your own goddess!

* * * * * * * * * * * * * * * * * * * *

ACT III

RE-CHOREOGRAPH

Two roads diverged in a wood, and I —
I took the one less traveled by,
And that has made all the difference.

— ROBERT FROST, "The Road Not Taken"

*E*ven though we may have choreographed the most spectacularly amazing life, sometimes we realize that the life we
are in isn't the life we want. And we have to make a decision:
whether to go forward on the path we are on and keep dancing
as best we can, to change paths entirely, or to figure out how to
integrate into our current reality those pieces of ourselves that
we left behind. Which, while scary, can also allow us to reap
rewards beyond our wildest dreams. Especially when the path
we choose is "the one less traveled by."

Whether it's choosing to divorce or to stay, have a baby or
not, keep the pension and profit sharing or go out on your own
and move to Hawaii, one thing's for sure: It's a decision that
only you can make, and as much as others may want to help or
support you in that decision, you are the only one who knows
how you feel inside. You are the only one responsible for your
successes or your failures. You are the only one who can decide
for you, because you are the one who has to live with the consequences.

I found my fetish, laughed out loud, and accepted unconditionally, which left me so gloriously happy that I knew I had
no choice but to re-choreograph my life into all that I suddenly
knew it could be. Which was equal parts thrilling and intimidating! Knowing that the path I was choosing, going from

lawyer to burlesque star and coach, was "the one less traveled by," I learned that the only way to navigate the negative, both within my own head and from external sources, was to trust fully in my own truth. And as long as I did, and as long as I remained committed to my own choreography, no matter how stressful or confusing things got, it would always work out perfectly in the end! Right?

CHAPTER 6

Re-choreographing My Life
with the Final Two Steps of FLAUNT!

*Y*ou know those moments when you sit back, look around, and think, *How did I get here? How is it even possible that this is my life?* Those moments happen a lot for me. There is no question in my mind that without *FLAUNT!* I would never have found my inner burlesque star or re-choreographed my life in such a scintillatingly authentic way. I had no idea that there were opportunities for women of my age to dance or perform, yet here I was!

And ironically, had I been introduced to burlesque in any other context, I might have rejected it as bizarre. Had I seen it only as an art form and not as a form of spiritual growth and personal development, I'd never have continued. Burlesque brought together everything I had ever done and loved and provided me a container that I could fit in with 100 percent accuracy and authenticity. No longer did I have to leave bits and pieces of myself behind. For the first time ever I saw exactly how all of my gifts, all of my desires, all of me could be integrated into a cohesive whole. I saw how I could show myself and be seen fully, as *me*.

It had all come together so perfectly, so spontaneously, that it was totally meant to be! Going forward, life would be so much easier than it had ever been before!

"We Go Together Like
Rama Lama Lama Ka Dinga Da Dinga Dong"

Some things are just a given, they go together so well. Bacon and eggs, peanut butter and jelly, staying late and taking on extra projects if you want a promotion, and moms being with their kids on holidays. No question, right? So how do we handle those inevitable situations that come up where there is truly no way to bring together everything that we need to bring together? We navigate, that's how! Just like we'd navigate across a crowded dance floor when the DJ plays our favorite song and we need to get out there and dance!

Whether at a wedding or a dance club, if you have been dancing, I'm certain you have had a similar experience. Your favorite dance song, which also happens to be everybody else's favorite dance song, comes on, and everyone rushes onto the floor, where they break out in wild, energetic dancing. But your group of friends is on the other side! Even though the actual distance is not that far, cutting across the dance floor to reach them is quite a journey. Squeezing between people, you get jostled, shuffled to one side or the other, and continually have to turn sideways to fit through the constantly shifting space. Oftentimes you get stepped on, elbowed, or bumped, or you may even have a drink spilled on you. Of course, going around the dance floor is also an option, but even that is not a straight shot. Typically you have to navigate around tables, chairs, staff, coats, bags, and other people.

My point is, no matter what, the journey is not easy. It takes longer than you think, you will be caught off guard by unexpected occurrences, and there are moments of frustration and irritation. But knowing that the song is going to last only three or four minutes, you persist, because dang it, you want to dance!

FLAU_NT! Step 4: Navigating the Negative

Dance is exactly what I wanted to do. Dance! Six months after my burlesque audition, my dance troupe got an invite from the producers of a festival at Harrah's casino. I looked at the calendar, saw that it was Easter weekend, and said no. I was a mom, and it was a holiday. That was it; I was out.

I hadn't even considered what we were doing for Easter or if my teenage children even cared about Easter anymore. I was just responding as I thought I should — and more precisely as I thought others expected me to respond. The limitation had been squarely within me. It had not come from others.

Here's how it would go. I'd excitedly tell my friends that my dance troupe was performing in Las Vegas but that I couldn't go. Without fail, everyone would ask me why, and I'd explain that (logically) I couldn't go because it was over Easter weekend. And also without fail, everyone would look at me like I had just grown a second head.

"How many people have the chance to dance in Vegas, ever?" one friend asked. "When you are eighty years old, are you going to bask in the glow of your memories from some random Easter, or are you going to bask in the glow of your memories of dancing in Vegas?"

Another friend pointed out that I had teenage boys and asked if they still got up early to hunt eggs. "No," I said. "Last year I woke them up at noon so we wouldn't be late to Easter dinner."

"So *why* aren't you going again?" she asked. "Didn't you say that your flight back would land at 8:30 in the morning? Will they even be up before you get home?"

I really couldn't answer, because they were correct. I was limiting myself based on my own negative beliefs. Instead of navigating, I was crashing myself needlessly into a roadblock of my own creation.

Feeling embarrassed, I asked my family if they minded if I snuck away on Easter weekend, assuring them I would be back in time for Easter dinner. Nobody criticized me or berated me for leaving on Easter weekend. In fact, they suggested we bump dinner back by an hour just to make sure I wasn't rushed! Why had the martyr in me been so certain that I couldn't work this out? The perceived roadblocks had been my own, created by my own incorrect assumptions and beliefs. It was others who saw something in me that I had not seen in myself, who helped call me out on my own limited ideas and encouraged me to navigate my own negativity so I could dance in Vegas and live my dream.

Little did I know that the real navigation had just begun!

The plane touched down and the whirlwind began. I barely had time to drop off my bags in my room and it was time for the photo shoot. The others had arrived in Vegas the night before and were wide-awake, perky, and perfectly made-up with pinup hair and makeup. I, on the other hand, looked exactly like I had been traveling all night. Because I had. Slapping on some makeup as my friends did what they could with my hair, I realized that I could either back out of the photo shoot or let go and enjoy the moment. Even though it was far from what I envisioned, I chose to let go of perfection and enjoy.

Next up, a fashion show where the five of us were to model twenty-five different outfits during an eight-minute segment. Taking into consideration the time required to walk on and off the gigantic stage, most of our costume changes were less than a minute long. As the number progressed, our neat stacks of costumes turned into crumpled heaps on the floor and our brains frazzled. During the last costume change, I heard someone whisper loudly, "Nipple." And then louder, "NIPPLE!" I looked up in time to notice that the costume of the dancer who was up next had not been pulled down correctly, and her nipple was fully exposed! Just as she stepped onstage, another dancer grabbed her dress and yanked it into place! Disaster was averted and we were an undeniable hit.

Elated and exhausted, we went back to the hotel to sleep and prepare for our early-morning tech rehearsal the next day. Tech rehearsal is where performers get ten minutes of stage time to run through their routine, giving them the chance to see how their number works on the actual stage and allowing the tech crew the chance to figure out lighting and sound. The audio crew couldn't get our music to work, and because the stage was so much larger than our practice space, our placement was all messed up. At last, our music began to play, but no sooner had it started than it was shut back off and the next performer was called up. Our time kept running, regardless of the fact that our music hadn't. We were going to have to perform without ever having done a full run-through!

Off to the dressing room we went, where we crowded around the mirrored closet doors, altering the formations as best we could, but before we could finalize the changes, it was time to change into our identical 1950s-inspired outfits — dark blue high-waisted shorts and red-and-white polka-dot halter tops that tied around our necks and at our backs — and head out to the car show, where we were working a booth. Putting on our tops, we discovered that no matter what we did, our strapless bras showed. Horribly! Our only option was to go braless, which was not comfortable.

To make matters worse, I had forgotten to pack sandals. All I had were my tennis shoes and my dance shoes, which were brand-spanking-new. No time like the present to break them in! As we hurried to the car show, breasts bouncing, our nipples started to rub painfully against the fabric of our shirts. Laughing about last night's near *nipple slip*, we held our arms over our chests to prevent our boobs from bouncing, but it didn't help. The fabric of the tops had never been washed. In fact, it had been starched, repeatedly, and was heavy and stiff like sandpaper.

By the time our shift in the 102-degree parking lot of the car show had ended, two of the women's nipples were bleeding, and I was hobbling. There wasn't time for all of us to shower, so we had to make do and start in on our elaborate pinup hairstyles. Dirty hair holds a style better anyway, right? Looking far better than we felt, with our fake lashes, fake hair, makeup, and costumes, we made our way back to the theater, much quieter than the day before.

I had blisters on the bottom of each big toe, the tops of my pinky toes, and the inside of my right heel. The one on my heel was the size of a quarter and seemed to keep growing. While I was limping around backstage, one of the stagehands offered me some moleskin, which I gratefully accepted. Cutting myself a generous piece, I stuck it right onto my blister!

"Um, you're supposed to stick that to your shoe, not to your blister!" he said, appalled by what I had just done. Of course I knew that! I was so frazzled that I had done it wrong! I tried to pull the moleskin off my foot, but it wouldn't budge and I was out of time. I buckled up my shoe and stood up. Oh! That was so much worse! The moleskin tightened up the space, making the shoe push harder against my blister. Nothing I could do now. The show was starting, and *I was about to dance in Vegas! I WAS ABOUT TO DANCE IN VEGAS!*

I hurried onstage and froze into my first position. The voices in my head wouldn't stop chattering, reminding me not to forget this foot position, to do my final cross on count three, not count two. My heart hammering away in my chest reminded me that this routine, this whole experience, was about heart. I had fought so hard to be able to be here that I didn't want to miss it by being too much in my head. I wanted to bask in the stage lights and hear the music, the vocals, and the roar of the crowd. I wanted to feel the strain in my body when I pushed it to do new things and the sweaty-palmed rush of nerves before each performance. Comfort or discomfort, I wanted to feel it all, not be so distracted that I missed the joy of being where I was at.

Which was a mistake I had made more often than I cared to admit, and which I think most of us are guilty of; that is, we get so busy making sure things get done right that we miss the joy of the actual experience. I didn't want to do that. I wanted to enjoy myself fully and absorb the experience of dancing — onstage — in Las Vegas. I breathed in, let go, and heard and felt the music. I tuned in to the passion and joy of everyone dancing around me and the thrill of moving in unison. Sure, it had taken a lot for me to get to this moment, but moments like these were worth the hassle. I hadn't quit, and now, here I was!

My little duet part was coming up, and I couldn't wait to get out in front and show off a bit! Right on cue, I moved forward, and just as I was about to do my most powerful kick, I felt a gush of warmth pour into my shoe. I dropped the kick a little but kept dancing. My blister had burst! The pressure was relieved and, like that, my foot felt better! How ironic that increasing the pressure, making my foot more uncomfortable in the short run, was the very thing that caused my blister to burst, providing me with instant relief! Which was kind of like this whole trip, and the way one challenge after another kept popping up. Backing off wouldn't have helped. It was only by *navigating the negative*, pushing through each challenge, increasing the pressure, that I found relief and was finally able to say, "I danced in Vegas!"

FLAUNT! Step 5: Trusting My Truth

Think back to the "Living in the Glitter" exercise and how truth can be subjective. Not only is our external reality subjective, but our internal reality can be as well. Layer our self-doubt and confusion about who we are and what we like to do with everyone else's ideas about who we are and what we should do, and it's no wonder we have such a hard time choreographing our own lives! But here's the thing. We are the only ones who know what's going on inside us. We are the only ones who can ascertain with any certainty what is valid for us. And the only way to do that is to cut down the external noise, turn within, and trust that what we find is right for us. Even if it's not what we expect!

Six months after my trip to Vegas, I was standing backstage at the House of Blues in New Orleans, looking at the walls, which were covered with the names of every performer who had performed there. Everywhere I looked I was reminded that I was walking the same path that Johnny Cash had on his way to this very same stage. It humbled me, yet it also made me proud to know that I was one of the ones who had said yes and trusted my own truth.

It wasn't that I was famous by any stretch of the imagination; it was just that I dared to say yes to what was in my heart, and that "stretch" had brought me here. Granted, I sometimes still had to fight with myself, to remind myself that taking risks and making myself a priority was my right, not a luxury, but I was learning to accept unconditionally all that I felt called to do. My heart was open to whatever was in front of me, and it led me to this moment, here in New Orleans — to the exact same stairwell where so many others who had taken risks had stood before me.

My mind went back to my exodus from the corporate world, when my coworker told me I was letting down working women everywhere by leaving the rat race and becoming a stay-at-home mom. If she could only see me now! I laughed at how horrified I imagined she would be at my recent determination to carry on the burlesque lineage instead of her version of the stereotypical working woman's lineage. Perhaps conforming to that stereotype was her truth, but this was undeniably mine.

Society said that a middle-aged mom, lawyer, and coach shouldn't do what I was doing. But I did it anyway. Not to rebel or to create a fuss but because it was *my* truth to do so. To dance my own dance with wild abandon. My actions were rooted in trusting my own truth and would hopefully validate others who wanted to live their lives their way.

No longer was I *just mom* or *his wife*. I was Lora. And no matter which roles I took on, from this point forward I would play them as only Lora could play them. And what felt the best to me was knowing that I would never go back to being a supporting player in somebody else's drama. I was my own burlesque star! This was my life, created by me, and I was going to live exactly as my soul wanted me to live. My light was turned on high, and I was not going to go back to living in the dark.

Even though I wasn't sure what life was going to look like going forward, I knew that trusting in my truth would get me wherever I needed to go. After all, could I have ever planned or predicted my midlife foray into burlesque? But here I was, and it fit perfectly. The rest of my life was going to be up to me. I could no longer rely on others to rescue me or tell me what to do, and that was equal parts intimidating and thrilling!

I mean, really! The idea of moving forward and choreographing my own life forevermore felt kind of overwhelming, too. When could I relax? I had already *done it* and broken free, right? I went from lawyer to burlesque star! Yeah! I won! Now what? Part of me wanted to be given a road map for the rest of the journey. To have the rest of my life neatly laid out for me, so I could once again plod mindlessly along, doing what I was supposed to do. But there was no road map for the journey that I was on. My journey was mine, it was of my own creation, and inside I knew that I was ready.

Burlesque, with its focus on humor and female-dominated power, gave me explicit permission to live confidently and joyfully exactly as I was. Funny, but it was breaking the rules through a somewhat taboo art form that empowered me in ways I hadn't known I needed empowering. Seriously, though, if I was brave enough to get up onstage, *at my age* and *with my body*, and take off my clothes in front of a thousand people, there wasn't anything I couldn't do. The thought of flashing the judge from my student-law-office days sprang briefly to mind, making me chuckle. Can you imagine how different my life might have been if I had known the power of choosing and validating myself sooner?

Thinking back on my life, on all I went through when I hid myself and dropped out of college, when I covered myself to succeed as a lawyer, when I suppressed myself as a wife and mother, I saw that there were five distinct steps I had taken every time I reclaimed myself. I found my fetishes and allowed myself to have fun and laugh out loud at myself and at life. I accepted who I was and what I liked, as well as everyone and everything around me, unconditionally and without judgment. I navigated the negative and developed a can-do attitude, seeing challenges as puzzles to be solved instead of walls that would stop me. And, above all, I trusted squarely in myself and my truth.

My truth was abundantly clear. And I knew that I was now brave enough to *trust* that truth. I was done with endless self-help programs, fruitless manifesting, and nonspecific vision boards championing ideas I couldn't quite grasp and didn't really understand. It was time to release the idea of what I thought my life was supposed to look like and to reveal myself for exactly who I was. Burlesque dancer and Life Choreographer® might not be *real* career options for others, but they were for me! Because they were my truth. And I couldn't wait to begin!

That is the story of how I found my *FLAUNT!*

CHAPTER 7

Re-choreograph Your Life with the Final Two Steps of FLAUNT!

Whether it's letting go of a bad relationship, moving out of a toxic work environment, or coming out in some regard to your family and friends, I have a sneaking suspicion that, like me, you, too, have found yourself teetering precariously on the precipice of change a time or two. Where you know where you want to go, but the journey to get there seems overwhelming to the point that it sometimes seems easier to quit. So instead of committing to that change and risking failure, you sometimes look for an excuse that justifies quitting.

By reading this book and working through the exercises, you have potentially undergone some significant transformation. You have shed masks, had some glittery fun, found your joy, and allowed a little magic into your own life. Perhaps you have learned how to deconstruct bits of your thinking and re-write pieces of your programming, and are more aware of your self-imposed limitations. You have looked at your life as a series of burlesque routines with music, costumes, masks, props, and choreography. You might also have seen where some of those pieces need a little upgrade!

With fresh eyes, a metaphorically naked body, and a pure heart, it's time to listen to your own soul and step into your raw truth. Your divine destination, your authentic self, is right there underneath, waiting to be revealed. Your magical, elusive life purpose is right there, too, ready to be embraced. All that you've been looking for but have never quite been able to see is now coming into view. You can navigate your way there, or you can look for excuses to quit.

You are the only one who can navigate your way there, to the end of the song. Are you going to dance this dance or stop short? Despite some similarities, nobody has been on your exact journey before. We all live our own labyrinth, so to speak. There is no one-size-fits-all choreography, and that's a good thing. Even if it feels kind of scary. Because dancing freestyle and creating your own steps is the only way to make sure that the journey is wholly your own. Re-choreographing your life means mastering the final two steps of *FLAUNT!* — Navigate the Negative and Trust Your Truth — and being brave enough to never quit. Because when you keep on doing what you love, glorious things beyond your wildest imagination will occur. Ask me, I know!

I believe that you know a lot about yourself. Even if you aren't ready to admit it. Are you going to build your dreams and live your sparkle, or are you going to look for excuses to quit?

FLAUNT! Step 4: Navigate the Negative

Although there are parts of *FLAUNT!* that are fun and giddy — like getting back in touch with our childhood dreams and desires, remembering how to play, looking for magic in the everyday, turning our lives into a burlesque, finding our fetish, and laughing out loud — *FLAUNT!* also addresses the fact that life, like any performance, does not always flow exactly as we intend. We can't always lead. Sometime we must follow. And knowing when to lead and when to follow helps us reach our destination more quickly and efficiently.

Securely in the arms of our partner, excited to show off our new salsa or ballroom skills, we envision our spin across the dance floor to our favorite song being like something out of a movie. In reality, we inevitably encounter other couples who get in our way, drinks spilled on the floor, skips in the music, a move we weren't expecting our partner to lead us into, and a hundred other distractions or hiccups. No matter how well rehearsed our choreography, something always knocks us off course.

Navigating the negative means doing whatever is required to get to our desired destination. Whether it's going around, over, or through things in order to reach the desired end, it is rarely ever a simple process of moving directly from point A to point B. Navigation is an active process, requiring us to respond to the feedback we receive and obstacles we encounter and to adjust our course accordingly. Of course, we can have our plan, our choreography, but there are also times when it is necessary to pull back, go with the flow of the present moment, laugh, and enjoy the ride. Chicken Dance, anyone?

Navigating the negative means knowing what to do when the unexpected happens, and how to gracefully ride the line between following the choreography we know and ad-libbing with enough confidence to get us successfully through. If you have ever been thrust into a line dance that you don't know, you'll understand exactly what I'm talking about here. The first few rounds you are off beat, stepping, turning, clapping, or tapping at mostly the wrong times, but halfway through the song you are doing the Electric Slide or Macarena-ing like a pro!

In every situation, we must balance our skills, moves, and direction with those of the people around us, honoring our full expression of self, letting our light shine as brightly as we desire, while at the same time honoring others and their individual expressions and paths. Successful navigation, both on and off the dance floor, requires us to be mindful of the times when we try too hard to control and direct every little detail. Because here's the thing: it is only when we are in a state of openness, connection, and joy that we can accept all that the Universe brings our way. Despite wishing for concrete rules to follow, there is no one right way to navigate, and no two journeys are ever the same.

Because we are products of our environments, we tend to get locked into the belief that there is one proper way to do things. It's like this: Somebody, somewhere along the line, taught us the four-count box step and told us that was dancing. Not that the box step was wrong, but it was the only dance step we knew. We may have learned variations on that step in terms of speed, style, and flair, but no other dance steps were taught. Believing that this dance was *the* way to dance, we internalized that step and began our journey.

And then somebody played a three-count waltz! We fell off course, we couldn't get our four-count box step to work no matter what we tried, and we were mystified and lost! We had done everything *right* and had followed the steps properly, so what happened? Instead of re-choreographing, navigating, and figuring out alternative ways of going on, modifying our steps, making it work, learning new skills, or asking for different music, we got discouraged or erroneously thought that the Universe was telling us that our desires were not meant to be, and we quit. When all it was really doing was telling us it was time to learn a different dance.

Nonattachment

There are many ways for us to learn the art of navigating the negative. One of those ways is to practice the yogic concept of nonattachment, which is releasing attachment to the outcome and focusing only on the quality of the action taken. Because what is the only thing we can control? Our actions! Not the outcome. If we bake cookies that fall and don't rise, the practice of nonattachment emphasizes our loving intention to provide something delicious for our family — not on the ugly, flat cookies. Practicing nonattachment keeps our focus on positive intention, bolsters our ego, releases us from self-judgment, and maybe even provides us with an opportunity to learn what we otherwise could have missed.

For example, regarding the cookie situation, focusing on the intention, rather than on the outcome, means that we might willingly expose our cookie error to the world, and thereby learn that high-altitude baking requires more flour! If we focus on and shamefully hide (or eat in secret) all our flat cookies, we totally miss an opportunity for learning.

To navigate the negative means managing expectations. How would our ability to handle setbacks be different if we were taught to stay fluid and flexible instead of being taught to follow precise directives? Kind of like being taught *how* to think, as opposed to *what* to think? What if we grew up knowing that life was filled with many challenges and that experiencing challenges did not mean we were doing it wrong? What if we embraced challenges as puzzles or games, and we enjoyed the process of figuring out which dance steps went to which songs? Do we do a rumba, cha-cha, tango, waltz...or is now the right time to whip out the tap shoes? *Whee!* Staying alert and curious, while knowing that feeling discouraged and getting it all wrong is a normal part of living, helps us tremendously to release our attachment to a precise outcome and enjoy the ride.

Not all obstructions are external. Many things blocking our path arise from within and are based on fear. Fear of failure, fear of rejection, fear of success, and fear of what will happen if we move outside ourselves and our boxes. When I went to my first pole class, there was nothing external in my way. I bought the class, drove to the studio, and had the proper attire, and the instructor and class members were all there, ready to accept and teach me. It was my own litany of fears that almost kept me from walking in the door. Fear of the unknown, fear that I wasn't young enough, strong enough, or fit enough. Not to mention my fear of loving pole and having to explain to others what I was doing if I decided to continue.

It was the same with my first burlesque audition. The people seemed hostile, and the dances felt like they were over my head. But they weren't. I conquered my fear, navigated the situation the best I could, did some dances well, and failed at others. And in the end, I succeeded enough to get what I wanted. I learned that the people there weren't hostile and competitive at all. My perception of them was a reflection of my insecurity, not their actual attitudes. They were focused on their own dancing and their own insecurities as much as I was on mine. It was my own fearful projections that made them seem unfriendly. Ouch! With hindsight and clarity, is there a time this may have happened to you as well?

In both instances, when I let go of attachment to the outcome and focused on me, my intention, my joy, my attitude, and all that I truly could control, the results were actually better than I could have anticipated! When we have no attachment to outcome, we are free to receive unexpected lessons and blessings that flow from what may otherwise be perceived as an accident. Sometimes, a mistaken outcome is actually better than the outcome we had planned.

My inadvertent purchase of a boudoir photo shoot was definitely no cosmic accident! That one simple "mistake" led me to pole, which led me to burlesque, which led me to being able to synthesize all aspects of my life and personality in ways that I could never have done on my own. Had I known at the time what would come from clicking that one little "buy now" button, I wouldn't have wasted a moment stressing over what I had just done.

The Stripper's Nightmare

Okay, despite all that talk about how mistakes are really golden opportunities to learn, who else loves it when things go exactly as planned? It's the best, isn't it? Sometimes I get so in the mode of checking off one box after another, of moving through my day with the frenzied excitement of accomplishment, that I slip into a state of weird paralysis when things go wrong.

I know that all the other perfectionists are totally hearing me right now. For me, I can get so locked up in my own head-space, fixating on how thing "should have" turned out, that I lose track of my goal, my desired outcome, and the fact that there's more than one path that leads me there. It's not until I get out of my head, out of what "should" be, and into my body and what actually *is* that I'm able to break free and move ahead.

"The Stripper's Nightmare" is a classic burlesque routine that can break us out of that weird, locked-up paralysis and make us laugh. It reconnects us with our heart and gets our creative juices flowing once again so we can kick it back into high gear and solve those pesky unforeseen problems without missing too many beats.

Remember that burlesque routines are microcosms of life

and that burlesque is a parody. "The Stripper's Nightmare" is a comedic routine that performers have done for years, and it's the perfect illustration of how to navigate the negative without quitting, freezing, or being swallowed up by life's inevitable problems.

As performers of any kind know, when something goes wrong onstage, it is their job to re-choreograph on the spot and cover those errors with such deftness that the audience never knows that anything went awry. And even when the audience becomes aware of the problem, consummate performers handle those situations with such tact that the enjoyment of the show is not compromised.

And now I bring you… "The Stripper's Nightmare"!

Picture a beautiful, elegant, and graceful woman, dressed to the nines in a long gown, heels, gloves, a fur stole, a glorious feather headpiece, and dripping with jewels. She floats confidently onto the lush stage, accompanied by classic big-band music, and slowly and deliciously peels off her gloves with the power and control of a lioness. *Ahhhh, she's simply sublime!* But as she twirls her fur stole seductively, she knocks off her feather headpiece, messing up her hair and making her previously elaborate hairstyle lopsided and rumpled. *Oops!*

She recovers masterfully, dancing and sashaying across the floor while teasingly removing her jeweled belt, which snaps up and hits her in the face as the too-tight elastic is released. She keeps moving, pretending not to notice, and reaches her hand up to flirt with the tasseled end of her zipper. The zipper of her sequined gown begins to melt down her back, but then it gets stuck! It's caught on something, and no matter how hard she tugs, it won't move. No worries, she gives a sly wink and provocatively slides her dress down over her shoulders and hips. Slowly, mesmerizingly, she reveals a gorgeous vintage bra, but as the dress slides down, she gets stuck awkwardly, with one arm caught in the sleeve, wedged at her side.

After a couple of too-hard tugs, which only make things worse, she smiles, gathers the dress, which is now pooling around her ankles, and saunters toward her ornate chaise lounge. But because the dress is now too long, her heel gets caught in the hem and she stumbles, hopping along uncoordinatedly.

Safely seated, she regains her composure, frees her stuck arm with an undignified pop, and bends down and frees her caught shoe. With her arm now freed, she works her way out of the dress and unhooks and removes her bra. But as she slides it toward the floor, the hooks catch on her fishnets. Bra dangling from her leg, she gives an exasperated smile; stands up, one shoe on, one shoe off; and finishes her dance, bra dangling at her side and hair falling in her face.

There are sometimes situations in life where, like "The Stripper's Nightmare," literally everything that can go wrong does. Despite our best efforts, we are sometimes unable to hide or cover any of it. All we can do is navigate the negative, keep on smiling, and trust that, despite all outward appearances to the contrary, everything is exactly as it should be.

What I like about this routine, besides the obviously co-medic fun, is that it demonstrates the power and tenacity of if-then reasoning, which is the ideal framework to use when we find ourselves stuck or paralyzed by uncertainty. *If the zipper gets stuck, then what do I do? If my hair falls out, then what? If the goal is to be nearly naked by the end of the routine, how am I going to ensure that I meet my goal, no matter what gets in the way?*

Asking, and then answering, the question "If [whatever happens], then what?" gives the mind the chance to pre-pare and plan for the unexpected and allows the brain the opportunity to preview, or try out, various options so as not to get locked into one way of thinking. Why is this valuable? Remember hypnosis? Our subconscious minds do not know the difference between fantasy and reality. When we think through different situations in our minds, we make those options *knowns* instead of *unknowns*, and they become less of a threat, less stressful to implement. Working through challenges mentally prepares us and makes us more comfortable with and capable of working through challenges in real life. Who doesn't want to make life easier?

If-Then Practice

Let's give it a try! Begin with a goal that's not too complicated, just so you can practice and see how this works for you. Start with your end point in mind, assess where you are right now, and come up with the steps necessary to reach your desired destination. *Bam!* There you have it, your initial road map, your base choreography. If your end goal is making spaghetti, your road map might include finding a recipe, shopping for the required ingredients, and boiling the pasta. Looking at the steps, can you identify places where things might go wrong?

In sales they call this *countering the objection*, and the goal is to recognize and counter possible objections before customers have the chance to raise them. In law, they call it *inoculating the jury*. If a lawyer has to put a witness on the stand who has something that could make them less credible in the eyes of the jury, it's better to present those compromising facts up front, rather than have opposing counsel spring them on the jury after they have begun to trust the witness.

For example, if the star witness has a DUI, it's much less alarming for the jury to hear about it as that witness is being introduced, perhaps like this: "I'd like to bring Mr. Jones to the stand. Mr. Jones, have you ever had a DUI?" And then Mr. Jones can admit to, and possibly explain the facts surrounding, his DUI. Then the questioning can proceed, and the jury can get to know, like, and trust Mr. Jones despite the fact that he had a DUI. Which is much less shocking than having the information sprung on them by opposing counsel, leaving them blindsided and unsure of their ability to further trust Mr. Jones.

I hear you asking, "What about positive thinking? Isn't this just creating problems where none exist?" No, this is not throwing up blocks where none exist. It is simply looking ahead for icebergs. Remember the *Titanic*? What might have changed about that voyage if someone had looked ahead and planned what they were going to do in the event of an iceberg?

If we see an iceberg, *then* what? Perhaps we can slow down, turn, stop, load the lifeboats to max capacity…you get the idea. No matter what the situation, there are always more options than we initially recognize, and giving ourselves the opportunity to think through plausible solutions in advance is usually a pretty good idea.

For each step in your choreography, look for potential icebergs and ask yourself, *If* [iceberg], *then what?* and let your creative answers flow. This is more like a brainstorming session than an actual strategy session, so don't shut down any options as being unrealistic just yet. If the store is out of spaghetti noodles, then what? Fusilli? Rigatoni? Try spaghetti squash? Make your own pasta? Head to a different store? Borrow pasta from a friend? Purchase pasta from a restaurant? What are your options?

If the stove won't turn on, then what? Can you use the microwave and still make this work? Can you boil water in a hot pot? A coffeepot? The oven? Head to the neighbor's house? Build a fire over the firepit? In the fireplace? Call an emergency repair person?

I know the spaghetti example is simplistic, but simplistic examples are a good place to start, because they illustrate the fact that there are way more options out there than we probably ever stopped to think about. Be ridiculous in brainstorming your options, please! Ridiculousness and genius are often closely related. One hot summer I actually cooked a frozen pizza on the hood of my car. And it worked perfectly! Ridiculous option or genius solution? I'll let you decide.

What's really good about if-then thinking is that in the process of thinking through a wide variety of possibilities, we keep our brains flexible, creative, and forward moving.

Asking ourselves *If* _____, *then what?* prepares us for many possibilities, gives us the opportunity to plan in advance, and provides insight that we may not otherwise have had. Because (words of wisdom coming up here) the only thing we can control in life is our reaction. We know life is inherently uncontrollable, so it behooves us to accept unconditionally and navigate the negative, in order to stay nimble and reach our desired goals. While changing external factors is often beyond our control, taming our own internal negativity *is* always something that we can control. Like the *Titanic*, we can't change the iceberg, but there's plenty we can do to navigate around it.

The Long Drive Home

A scenario I often take my clients through to help break them out of their own limited thinking is what I call "The Long Drive Home." I ask clients to imagine their drive home from work and what they would do if there is a terrible accident and one of the roads is closed. Or if the road is under construction and there is a detour. Or if a microburst hits and there is some pretty intense rain. Or if *all* that happens on the same drive home.

Not once, not ever, has a client told me that they would quit. That they would get out of their car, leave it by the side of the road, and not go home again. Not once has anyone ever told me that their experience would make them realize that getting home *wasn't in the cards, wasn't meant to be,* or *was just a pipe dream.* Without fail, every single client comes up with a way to make it home. Even if they have to spend an unexpected night in a hotel, they all eventually go home. Despite delay, detours, or stopping and waiting out the storm.

So, why is it different for us when we pursue our dreams or incorporate fetishes and fun in our lives, and things get a little difficult? *I guess it just wasn't meant to be!*

Thank you, Sir Alexander Fleming, accidental discoverer of penicillin, for taking time to look at your yucky contaminated and discarded petri dish and realize that the mold growing inside said petri dish was killing the bacteria around it! I am so glad that you didn't catapult into self-judgment over your continued failure to create the wonder drug you were trying for and stomp tearfully home with a pint of ice cream and box of Thin Mints tucked under your arm so you could binge-watch Netflix and convince yourself that you were in the wrong line of work altogether.

Even without having personally met you, I know you are more than worthy and more than capable of achieving your dreams. I also know that you have perseverance and gumption and don't really believe that you deserve last place in your own life. So what is it that makes you so willing to let your own dreams die before they even take flight?

Whether it's fear of failure or fear of success, that fear is likely in your own thinking, and is not real at all. I mean, really.

You've accomplished a lot in your life. Did you really expect your biggest, brightest dream to be the easiest to accomplish? Let's persevere for ourselves at least as vigorously as we'd persevere for others, shall we?

Back to the *Titanic*. Icebergs aren't positive or negative. They are neutral. It's the circumstances surrounding them that make them positive or negative. Like any of the things that pop up in our lives, they just *are*. It's our judgment around them that makes them either positive or negative. If we are on an Alaskan cruise, we label icebergs as *good*. If we are on the *Titanic*, we label icebergs as *bad*. But really, they are just icebergs. There's nothing personal or negative about anything that gets in our way. Detours, accidents, roadblocks, and bad weather. They just are. Whether we navigate around storms, icebergs, or costume malfunctions, our job is to find a way. The ocean is vast and wide, and there are a million different ways to get from point A to point B. How are you going to get there? Navigate the negative, that's how!

What would your life be like if you navigated every negative situation in your life with simple if-then thinking? Where would you be if you quit obsessing about the one or two ways you were metaphorically unable to get home and instead found one of the many other viable routes? How would things be different if you saw the things blocking your path as simply things to navigate around and you quit taking them personally? If _____, then what? You know the destination. Home is waiting. Now dance your way there!

FLAUNT! Step 5: Trust Your Truth

Trust is relying on someone or something that we aren't able to see, or that hasn't yet come to pass. We don't need to be perfect, enlightened, or *already there* in order to trust in our truth and boldly live our sparkle. Trust means knowing that however we are and whatever we desire is exactly right for us. We don't need to worry, or even figure out, how to get where we want to be; we only need to trust that we will get there. Trusting in ourselves means being aware that even when we can't see ourselves clearly, even when we cover certain aspects of our identity or live out roles that aren't completely authentic to who we are, we know that our inner core remains unchanged.

Truth is, quite simply, the state of being as we are. Our true essence *is* our true essence. It doesn't matter if we believe in it or not. Even when we don't believe our truth is what it is, it still is.

It makes no difference what others believe or don't believe about you and your truth, either. No matter how powerful or authoritative another person's opinion might be, it can't change the truth of who you are. Sure, you can modify or cover your truth to be more in line with what someone else tells you to be, but the modification of self does not change your innate truth.

Trusting Travesties: When We Trust Others More Than Ourselves

Trust is powerful. Whether it is in ourselves, another person, or a situation, the act of trusting makes us vulnerable. Yes, trusting the wrong person or situation can lead to suffering, whereas trusting the right person or situation can set us free, light our whole world on fire, and provide connection, support, and joy. But here's the catch. Whether we trust or distrust a person or a situation and whether the outcome is positive or negative, it all boils down to our ability to trust in ourselves. It has nothing to do with other people and everything to do with us!

Confused? Let me explain. If we trust in another and they

burn us, we blame them. It's their fault, not ours. They are the bad person who did us wrong. If we trust in someone and glorious things happen, we love them! They become our savior, our guiding light! But in either event, the choice to trust or not to trust is our own. It all comes down to us, every time. To our own discernment and intuition.

Have you ever had a situation where you didn't listen to your intuition and you got burned? I have, and then I beat myself up for not listening! Trusting in your truth means using discernment and trusting that still, small voice inside, despite what your head may tell you, and then accepting the outcome unconditionally.

We are each in charge of maintaining our own integrity. Even when things go wrong, being able to say "I did exactly what I thought was right, and that's the best I can do" is the most we can do.

Which is the opposite of what I did when my dentist retired and sold his practice to a dentist whom I intuitively did not trust.

I am a longtime tooth grinder who struggles with sensitivity due to receding gums, so my former dentist routinely put a touch of bonding over the base of my most sensitive teeth. Even though this has always worked fine, the new dentist advised me to redo my bonding with a stronger material that would not have to be replaced as often. Although his suggestion sounded reasonable, I felt anxious and uncertain. As in unreasonably anxious and spine-tinglingly uncertain. Which I ignored.

Not wanting to insult his authority — he was the dentist, after all, not me — and not wanting to be an argumentative, "difficult" patient, I ignored my feelings. I suppressed the pins-and-needles sensation in my body and told myself I was being ridiculous. So when he whipped up his schedule and asked me if — or rather, *told* me — I could have my new bonding redone the next week, I agreed.

Over the next week I somewhat obsessively sought advice from friends and family, with everyone telling me that dental work was not that big of a deal and that I'd be much happier with more permanent bonding. Although my head agreed with what everyone was saying, I continued to feel really icky about the whole situation. I told myself I was experiencing an irrational fear of the unknown and that I should grow up and get a grip.

The day of my appointment I literally felt so nauseated that I considered canceling. But because I didn't want a charge for a last-minute cancellation when there was nothing *really wrong*, I braved on.

Sitting in the dentist chair, stomach clenched and hands gripping the armrests, I stoically opened my mouth as the dentist reached in and said that I'd feel a little pinch for the numbing shot. My mind spun and my heart leaped in my chest. A numbing shot? I'd never had one of those before. Why was he doing this?

I yanked back, alarmed, demanding to know why I needed a numbing shot since I had never had one before. Shaking his head patiently, he explained that dentistry should be comfortable. My job was to relax and let him do his work! Part of me was embarrassed, but part of me was on high alert. He continued poking around in my mouth, grabbing various tools and stuffing me with gauze. I closed my eyes and focused on my breath. Until I heard it: the drill! Reflexively, my arm shot up and I grabbed his wrist. Startled, he asked me what on earth I was doing. Really embarrassed and really numb, I mumbled that I was sorry, but my former dentist had never used a drill during this procedure, and I was really concerned.

Not quite so patiently this time, he explained that he used the drill to rough up the surface of the tooth so the material could adhere. If I wanted this done correctly, I needed to keep my arms down and relax so he could work. I ignored the sensations of panic coursing through my body and willed myself to obey, although the procedure seemed to go on and on, with more drilling and messing around than I had ever experienced before.

Finally it was over and I could sit up and examine my teeth, which looked fine. Too fine. In addition to the two teeth with the old bonding, he had fixed two more teeth as well! I felt irritated and violated, but looking at my pretty teeth, I felt petty voicing my complaint. Forever the good girl, I stuffed down my feelings of being taken advantage of and talked myself into believing that the lack of clarity and understanding about what was being done to my teeth was probably my own, not my dentist's. After all, my thoughts had been pretty spun up lately, and he was the professional. I reminded myself that bonding on teeth was not that big of a deal, and I rationalized that this new dentist was much more progressive than my former dentist had been. I decided to let it go but to find a new dentist going forward.

Fast-forward six months to my first visit with my new dentist, who asked me about the four odd fillings on the fronts of my teeth. *What? I didn't have any fillings!* I explained that in order to combat sensitivity, I'd had bonding on the fronts of my teeth and that my last dentist had used some sort of super bonding. Maybe that was what he was seeing? On the contrary, he showed me four fillings, pointing out where so much of the original teeth had been drilled away that he was fearful I'd eventually lose all four teeth!

Words were inadequate to describe my dismay — not only

at the idea of someday losing my teeth but because I *knew* in my heart all along that I was making a mistake when I had that procedure done. I failed to trust my instincts. And I was the only one to blame. Had the dentist done something wrong? Yes, I believe he had. However, it was ultimately my responsibility to trust myself and advocate for my beliefs. I had failed myself.

Failure to trust our truth leads us to seek answers outside ourselves, from other people, doctrine, or rules, instead of from within our own being. It's not that we should never seek advice from others. There are many situations where we are not the most qualified. Seeking counsel from trusted friends or advisors is always wise. It's just that we need to run all input we receive from others through our own minds. We need to use our power of discernment, listen to our own prayers, and trust how we feel about the information we receive. Our hearts and bodies are wise. They let us know when we are about to head in the wrong direction. Just like my dentist experience: everything in my body screamed out for me to stop, but I got stuck in my head and failed to trust in myself, and I suffered the consequences.

Being fully connected to our bodies is like having a Magic 8 Ball that's actually accurate. It puts us in touch with our intuition and our truth, and it's rarely wrong. Plus it feels good to be in touch with our own physicality! Being unselfconscious and comfortable in our own skin tends to make us equally comfortable and nonjudgmental around others. Think about that the next time you find yourself getting all judgy about other people. The times we criticize others are the times we feel the least comfortable and connected with ourselves.

Being in your own truth means you'll have the ability to hear, appreciate, and experience a wide variety of different opinions and beliefs without the need to adopt, reject, or correct any of them. When you are so confident, and comfortable with yourself, you are not threatened by those whose truth is different from yours, because you know that different opinions, beliefs, or truths can never affect your own.

The Truth of Your Body

When you feel the deep assurance of living your own truth, you no longer question yourself or fall into toxic self-judgment, because you know exactly who you are. Your body knows. Your heart knows. Your truth *is* your truth, and building your dreams and living your sparkle is the most natural thing in the world. Your truth is absolute for you because it's a part of your divine soul. You are perfect exactly as you are. Although our humanness can make mistakes, our souls cannot be wrong.

To determine if something is true for you, ask yourself how it makes you *feel*, as opposed to what you *think* you should do. Asking *Does this feel right?* requires you to pause and tune in to how the answer feels in your body. When the decision is in line with your truth, the sensations in the physical body are comfortable — notwithstanding the excited kind of anxiety or nervousness due to trying something new!

There is a difference between being nervously excited and dreadfully nervous, and as you tune in more, you will learn to feel the difference. When there is some aspect of the decision that is out of line with your truth, you will feel it in your body as well. Your heart may feel jumpy or sick, or your spirit might feel heavy.

Our bodies house our minds and our spirits, and even though we can mentally rationalize or justify our actions, we can never fool the innate wisdom of our bodies.

Take a minute and think about a time you were talked into

doing something you didn't want to do or knew was wrong. How did you feel? Can you pinpoint where in your body you sensed it and what that sensation felt like? Then think about a decision you knew was right for you and how that felt in your body.

Many of the women I coach talk about the sensations they experienced in their bodies right before getting married. Whether the decision they were about to make was right or wrong, pretty much all of them had a knowingness either way. While we can trick our minds into believing something that is not true, we can't fool our bodies. Our bodies always know.

Before going onstage I can get an adrenaline rush so big that I feel like I will either explode or throw up. But the nervousness in my body feels excited and thrilling in a good way! I care about what I'm about to do, and although I'm anxious because I want to succeed, because I'm about to put myself out there in a big, nearly naked way, I wouldn't trade that kind of nervousness for all the world!

Want to know more about interpreting your feelings? Yogalesque is my practice for tuning in to the physical sensations of my body so I can judge whether or not I am living according to my own truth. Yogalesque combines burlesque with the ancient wisdom of the chakra system. It helps me figure out my truth, based on what's happening in my body. Then, as I re-choreograph my life to be in alignment with my truth, Yogalesque helps me embody the authentic feelings I experience inside but am having a difficult time expressing.

Yogalesque

Maybe you consider yourself to be pretty enlightened and self-aware? As a coach who practices yoga and meditation and who has the lowdown on every mindfulness trick in the book, I like to think that I am. However, I can assure you that even though I know exactly what I'm supposed to do in order to stay calm, focused, present, and filled with joy in every situation I could possibly encounter, I don't.

I don't always do what I'm supposed to do. I get tired, flustered, grouchy — whatever — and I fail. Or more frustrating, for me, others don't behave in the way I think they should behave, and it completely throws me for a loop! Sometimes I get a case of runaway monkey mind that can't be stopped. I obsess and worry, and even though I know better, I fall into self-judgment and criticize myself for failing to do a better job. Which does not help. But, as usual, burlesque — more specifically, Yogalesque — does!

Yogalesque is the conscious, daily practice of aligning your body physically with the way you want to feel emotionally. It combines yoga, chakras, and the body's energy systems with the theater and dance techniques of burlesque, yoking together movement and emotion in order both to hear the wisdom of our bodies and to process, clear, and create our desired mental and emotional state. No, this is not woo-woo magic; this is innate, intuitive stuff that we all do every day, mostly without even realizing we are doing it. Let me explain how.

Body Language

Freeze, wherever you are at right now, and notice the positioning of your body. Where are your shoulders and spine? Are you slouched, hunched over, or droopy? Where are your hands and arms? Are your legs crossed? Are you leaning to one side, or are you leaning back?

The way we hold our body tells us volumes about our mental and emotional state. Bringing conscious awareness to our normal, natural physical behavior provides insight into where we may be experiencing blocks. When we slap a hand to our forehead, lower our head, and say, "I just can't see it," we *can't*. We are covering our third eye and looking down! When we fold our arms around our stomach and declare, "That makes me sick!" it actually *does*. When our hands fly to our chest and we "Oooooohhhhhh!" over a cute kitty video, we are literally feeling the love that is pouring out of our heart. Our innate, intuitive actions give away our internal truth without our conscious awareness!

Have you ever been self-conscious about a ginormous zit on your face and tried to hide it by pulling your hair forward or holding your hand *casually* in front of your face to block the monstrosity? Did it work? No, and being the stellar intuitive that I am, I'll tell you exactly why not. Everyone you came in contact with was magnetically drawn toward your zit. There was this intense eye-zit connection that frustrated the heck out of you, and you couldn't figure out why. It was because your body language told people, *There's something going on behind my hand! There's something magical and mysterious behind my hair! You don't want to miss this!*

Humans, whether we know it or not, are body-language experts — and humans don't want to miss out on cool stuff! If we think something is being hidden from us, we naturally assume it's something really cool or special, which arouses curiosity. So we try twice as hard to find out what it is!

When you are self-conscious of your flat chest or your large chest or your nose or your wonky eyebrows or unwaxed mustache, what do you do? You adopt body language that you believe conceals your perceived flaw. You might roll your shoulders slightly forward or stand at a bit of an angle so others can't see you head-on. But what you are unknowingly doing is drawing others' attention to the exact thing you are attempting to conceal.

When body language shows that we are hiding something, it broadcasts to others: *Come look for what I'm hiding!* Which is the exact opposite of what we intend. You know the phrase "hidden in plain sight"? Yeah, that's pretty accurate. If you don't want people to notice something, go ahead and show it off!

Not only are humans body-language experts; we are also experts at reading energy. Our thoughts and intentions create physical energy, and although we don't see energy with our eyes, we perceive it with our bodies. And the energy we perceive influences our behavior.

Not sure what I'm talking about? Have you ever walked into a room where people have been fighting and felt like you could cut the tension with a knife? Have you ever set foot in a location that felt so holy, so sacred, that it moved you to tears? Both times you were perceiving and responding to energy.

The Body-Emotion Connection

What do you do physically when you try not to cry? The tightness around your throat, neck, shoulders, and eyes can be overwhelming, throwing you right into hysterics.

For most of us, it's easier to stay in control if we consciously take some deep breaths, relax our shoulders, tilt our heads up, and stretch out our necks. We intuitively do things with our bodies that help us change our emotional state. When we straighten our spines, lift our heads, square our shoulders, and pull ourselves together physically, it pulls us together emotionally as well. This is the power of Yogalesque and how we change our emotions by altering the physicality of the body.

So, when negativity is spewing forth all around, instead of getting sucked into the fray and having our energy and spirit depleted, we can use Yogalesque and consciously place our body in a position that supports positivity, strength of character, and wisdom. We can tune in to what's really going on and use the body as a magnet to attract exactly what we want to attract.

Yoga

If you live on planet Earth, you probably have at least a vague understanding that yoga has something to do with chakras, which are the energy centers of the body. And if you don't live on planet Earth, I'm an intergalactic author and that's pretty amazing! Anyway, when we stretch and move different areas of the body, we also move the emotions and the energy located there. Which means moving the body physically helps us release stuck emotions or feelings. Which is kind of a cool life hack, because we can release and process some of our unpleasant emotions without having to think or feel our way through every little sordid and painful detail.

Let's begin with a basic description of the chakra system and the energy contained in the different parts of the body. That way you will have a handle on which emotions and feelings correspond to which areas of the body, and you will have a greater understanding of how to move your own body in order to facilitate and clear your own stuck emotions.

Chakra Shots

To visualize the chakras, pretend you are sitting cross-legged on the floor in a giant, multilayer Jell-O shot. Your spine is the center of the shot, and right atop your head is the fluffy whipped cream. The *root chakra* is the bottom layer of the Jell-O shot that you are sitting in, and it is strawberry, or red. It extends from the bottom of the shot to just under the belly button. This area deals with safety, instinct, security, grounding, and survival. Think of this chakra as being your very base connection to Mother Earth. It's primal energy, and like all chakras, it houses both the positive and the negative use of this energy.

The next layer of the chakra Jell-O shot is the *sacral chakra*, and it is orange. The orange spans from the top of the root chakra to a couple of inches above the belly button. This chakra deals with emotion, flow, flexibility, desire, pleasure, creativity, procreation, the sweetness of life, and our relationship with the outside world.

On top of that, in the solar plexus region is (shocker!) the *solar plexus chakra*. This lemon-yellow layer deals with personal power, laughter, joy, anger, and feelings of victimization or frustration. This is our willpower, the way we assert ourselves in the world, and our mental abilities.

Next, all around the heart, ribs, and shoulders is the green layer, which is the *heart chakra*. The heart, not surprisingly, is the center point of the Jell-O shot, and it deals with love, compassion, peace, and harmony. As the center point, it is the bridge between the earth and spirit, transformation and integration.

From the tops of the shoulders to over the throat and nose is the blue layer, the *throat chakra*, which represents the voice, communication, clarity, expression, and judgment. Turned too high, this can be seen as manipulation, arrogance, and dominance; turned too low, it can be timidity, fear, and swallowing our words.

The *third-eye* or *brow chakra* is a beautiful indigo color and spans from the throat chakra up over the eye and forehead region. This chakra represents clear vision, perception, knowledge, and intuition. It deals with openness, imagination, and creative vision — or a lack thereof.

Last, from the top of the head to a few inches above — right into the whipped-cream layer — is the *crown chakra*, which is a glorious lavender or white color. This chakra represents bliss, spiritual connection, pure consciousness, divine purpose, and personal destiny. Its energy reaches way up into the ethers. This is the chakra that literally pulls divine energy down through the rest of the chakras.

Now that you have a basic understanding of the energy and emotion in each area of the body, you can begin to *read* your own body language and movements, as well as those of others, garnering a deeper awareness of what's really going on within.

Add a little burlesque magic into the mix, and — wow! — you have the power to navigate and clear just about any kind of negative emotion, as well as the ability to joyfully move into disruptive situations, turn them squarely on their head, and create exactly the circumstance you desire. All because of Yogalesque and your confidence in trusting in your whipped-cream-and-Jell-O–covered truth!

Burlesque Basics

The grand, glorious, glitter-covered, and overacted charade of burlesque is one style of performance. In any performance (and life is a performance), performers are believable when there is congruence between their words and actions. When Meryl Streep delivers a gut-punching line, we believe it with every fiber of our being. Why? Because she uses her body and her energy to convey the emotion of the words she delivers. There is congruence between her words and her energetic and emotional bodies, and it's powerful.

Congruence in our own lives creates authenticity and be-lievability that is as fun to watch as it is to perform. We create congruence in our own lives when we align our words, emotions, actions, and thoughts. We all have doubts. We all freak out, get insecure, hold ourselves to impossible standards, and struggle through times when we can't get out of our own way. When we pretend we are fine but we really aren't, our actions are not always congruent with our feelings or emotions. When we act like we have it all under control but we don't, our actions may not be congruent with reality and thus we are not believable. Nor are we probably having much fun pretending that everything is hunky-dory. And despite what we might think, others are most likely not believing our little charade, either.

Burlesque is a physical art form that requires us to move physically and joyfully into that which scares us. Our doubts, insecurities, negativity — whatever our taboo might be — burlesque challenges us to uncover it all and put it boldly on display. Which is what makes burlesque so thrilling to watch — and to perform! And in that congruence, we are free.

Yogalesque's combination of ancient wisdom and the glittery extravaganza of burlesque is what gives us the ability to flip our own script and create our own congruence. Through Yogalesque we can change our internal situation by changing our posture, by consciously embodying our inner burlesque star.

Moving physically into the stance of the confident, clear, positive woman you are at your core causes your emotions and thoughts to follow suit. The alignment of your body, mind, and spirit with the woman you are deep in your soul tames the voices in your head and positively influences the way others perceive you. Similar to how performers can create a burlesque routine that provokes a certain response, you can use Yogalesque in life to create the emotions or feelings you desire, no matter what is going on externally.

Interested? Strap on some stilettos and I'll show you how to walk in those puppies!

• ● ● ● •

Chakra Walk

The foundational exercise of Yogalesque is the Chakra Walk, which is an exercise where we practice using our chakras and our bodies to convey emotion. It's not about acting as much as it's about feeling and reacting, so don't worry that you'll do it wrong. You can't. All it takes is doing your normal, natural, and intuitive movements but adding a layer of awareness about what you feel when you do those movements. Specifically, we focus on the emotions that are traditionally held in the seven chakras. Remember, though, that we all move and feel things differently, so don't get too locked into specifics. Just do you.

Find a spot where you can take a little walk. You can walk up and down your living room, bedroom, or hallway. I recommend doing this exercise where you have a mirror, because seeing yourself provides invaluable feedback! Stroll naturally, back and forth, and as you do, let me guide you through a series of first the negative and then the positive feelings associated with each of the seven chakras. Your job is to allow feelings to wash over you and let your body change as they do.

Begin with the root chakra. Moving your awareness to the legs, pelvis, and tailbone region, imagine, visualize, or pretend that you are in a tough survival situation. Money is nonexistent; you are hungry, tired, and scared. Your life or your safety is literally at stake; this is a fight-or-flight situation, and you are about to be physically attacked. What stance do you take? How does your movement change? Do you tuck tail and run? Do you gather energy deep within your pelvic floor and prepare to fight? Do you crumple or shrink? What happens to the align-ment of your body?

Now, flip that situation. Imagine being safe, secure, and powerful. Know that you have more money in the bank than you could ever spend, and let that security penetrate your en-tire being. You have food, clothing, and a rich connection to others. Notice how it feels to know that you are secure beyond measure. What changes in the way you walk, in the carriage of your head, shoulders, and spine? Does the length of your stride change or the power or the force with which you walk? What does your mouth do? How does your forehead feel?

Let that go. Move into the orange sacral region of your pelvis, belly, and lower abdomen. Walk as if you were a nun who has dedicated her life to spiritual service, who has lovingly committed herself to poverty, chastity, and obedience. Or move more into an old-fashioned, uptight, Puritanical view of physi-cal pleasure, where you feel dirty and disgusted even thinking about sex, sexuality, or the weakness of human desires. You are dry, uninspired, blocked, and bland. How does it feel to move that way? Tune in to the drudgery of life. What happens in your body and your movements? Do you feel a sneer, or are your lips pursed? What do your digestion and breath feel like?

Now, flip that script. Walk as if you look amazing, sensual, on the prowl. Feel confidence ooze from every pore. Enjoy the swish of your hips, the stretch of your spine. Reach up and touch your hair, your cheek, and feel the silky sensation of your breath pulling in through your lungs. Breathe in, smelling the divine scent of pleasure and joy that surrounds you. How does your movement communicate that you are a saucy, sensual being who loves her own sexuality, pleasure, and joy? Run your tongue over your teeth and lips, tasting and reveling in all sensation.

What are your eyes doing? How does your breath move your body? What is your smile like now?

Moving on to the solar plexus chakra, walk as if you were without any personal power or authority. Feel what it's like to be timid, shy, and slow. Like you really don't understand what's going on around you, and even if you did, you wouldn't be able to effect change.

Let all that go and now walk with awareness, assertiveness, and power. Feel an understanding of the interconnectedness of life and sense those connections all around you. Feel your brain snap into high gear. Feel your personal power, your ability to have an impact and make change. Open your solar plexus region by stretching and lifting your rib cage physically, breathing in possibility and strength. What has changed in your stride, your stance, your posture, and your alignment now?

You are halfway there. Allow yourself to return to a natural state for a moment before moving into the heart, the center point of your chakra system. For the heart chakra, move and walk as if you were utterly alone, miserable, and heartbroken. Feel the devastation of having no one to turn to, of being utterly and completely undeserving of love. Of being betrayed, unworthy, and broken. What happens in your body? To your arms?

Drop that and allow yourself to walk into love. The pure, divine love of spirit but also human love. Feel the love of those around you radiate in toward your heart, and feel the love within you radiate out toward all of humanity. Feel adored, a part of the universal whole, who is fully able to express and receive love without limitation or inhibition of any kind. Snuggle into the pure warmth of loving and of being loved. Notice what your body does.

When you are ready, move to the throat chakra and take note of the neck and throat region. Walk as a repressed, frightened woman, who could be beheaded for expressing even the hint of an opinion that was out of line with the majority. Move as one who has been silenced, who has nothing to say, and when she tries, she is not understood anyway. Feel the tangle of thoughts in your head, and how they are unable to travel down to your mouth without jumbling up and getting stuck. What does holding this thought do to your brow, your face, and your shoulders?

Release that and walk as one with a powerful voice and a clear message that is eagerly being revered by the world. Feel the clarity, how the words easily slide from your brain, out your mouth, and into the world. Look around, feel the brightness and impact of your words, and move as if you could see the amazing, positive changes they create in others. You are heard! How do you respond physically to this knowingness?

For the brow or third-eye chakra, become aware of your forehead. Feel and walk as one who is mired in confusion. Move as if everything you do is destined to fail because you just can't figure it out. You can't see the end result. There is no awareness of the impact of your actions or how to do things differently. You. Are. Stuck. How do you move, and what does your body instinctively do? Do you want to fold forward and put your head in your hands? Are you sinking in despair?

Now, walk with the purpose and direction of one who has knowledge and foresight and is destined for success. Walk like someone who knows what she wants and how to get it. Not only that, walk as if you could literally see the future. Pretend you are someone who can put mental feelers out into any situation and ascertain the best course of action no matter what. Feel the connection, the perception, and the resulting clarity. How does your body respond?

And last, be aware of the crown of the head, the crown chakra. Walk as if you are a piece of trash with no significance to anyone. Feel the darkness, the complete randomness and hopelessness of life. Death is imminent. Whatever you do doesn't matter anyway.

Finally, walk as if you were a pure, holy child of God. A fully spiritually connected, glorious being who could never be harmed, lost, or forsaken. Move as one who has ultimate purpose, passion, and joy. Walk as if you were fully connected to your own truth! How does that feel? What do you do differently than you normally do?

The Chakra Walk provides a glimpse into behaviors and movements that you intuitively and instinctively do when certain emotions arise. The Chakra Walk is your opportunity to catalog and remember the way you move your body when certain emotions are present. Going forward, you can pull out these postures when you wish to remind yourself of who you are and how you deserve to feel. Yogalesque is consciously using movement to provide congruence between your body and your emotions. It helps you stay in your own power and trust in your own truth, and is a tool you can use to find joy in all situations.

The next time you get thrown for a loop or knocked off your center and your self-worth or confidence takes a nosedive, choose movements that support your truth and the way you want and deserve to feel. Reground yourself in your own innate body movements and feel your emotions follow suit. Create congruence between your body, mind, and spirit. Choose movements that empower you and support your truth and experiment with how changing your body changes your mind.

Your Brand-New Season! (Get It? "Brand"?)

If you have spent great portions of your life wishing for a map to follow or an instruction manual to read, I've got you covered! In the final exercise, you are going to re-choreograph your life by writing out a screenplay for your future. But before you write your next chapter, you have to know what feelings or flavor you want to create. Many performers have a certain identity, or brand. They are comedic, athletic, slow and sultry, or vintage. What is the identity, or brand, of your life?

Who are you? Go back to your burlesque name. If you have not already done so, formulate a tagline. What does my name and tagline tell you about me? I'm Chakra Tease, the Sexy, Flexy Goddess of Zen. Who are you? What is your signature color? Do you have a motto? Are there any other distinct branding or identity elements that convey who you are and what you believe? Your identity comprises your past, present, and future. And although your present may have been determined by your past, it does not determine your future. Release the past and re-choreograph your future with intention and clarity.

• ● ● ● •

The Elements of Drama and Writing the Screenplay of Your Life

In writing a play or screenplay, whether for a TV show or movie, writers use the elements of drama in order to construct their story. The basic elements of drama are: setting, plot, characters, theme, and style:

- The *setting* is where the story takes place.
- The *plot* is the sequence of events that make up the story.
- The *characters* are the individuals in the story.

- The *theme* is the main idea or the lesson.
- The *style* is everything that gives the show a certain flavor or feel, such as the time period, the language, and the costumes, makeup, and behavior of the characters.

Think about different TV shows that have been on over the years: *Leave It to Beaver* in the 1950s, *The Dick Van Dyke Show* in the 1960s, *All in the Family* in the 1970s, *Family Ties* in the 1980s, *Home Improvement* in the 1990s, and *Desperate Housewives* in the 2000s. Although the setting (the family home), the plot (the adventures of a typical modern-day family), and the characters (mom, dad, kids, neighbors, and friends) are fairly consistent, the theme and the style of each show are vastly different. Each show was set in a different decade and a different part of America, giving them all distinctly different styles. While shows such as *Leave It to Beaver* had a theme that supported the correctness of the fifties status quo, *All in the Family* encouraged shaking up the status quo and accepting change.

Your life is like a three-part series, with season 1 being your past, season 2 being your present, and season 3 being your future.

In your mind, summarize the first two seasons of your life, thinking about the setting, plot, characters, theme, and style, before launching into a detailed screenplay for the third and final season. Specifically, what are the unifying themes, lessons learned, and values portrayed? What issues, if any, arose repeatedly season to season? Was there a definitive shift from one season to another, where you took more ownership or control over your life or where the style or theme changed over to something entirely different? List the various roles you have played.

Will they shift in season 3? Are any roles or characters

written out of the script altogether? Do the changes you make affect the other characters? At the very end of season 3, is there regret? Are there more changes you wish you had made that you didn't? Is the ending a peaceful, happy resolution?

Ponder the following sample hypotheticals to see how changing just one element changes the screenplay entirely.

Setting

How would your favorite show or series be different if the families portrayed had lived in a different time or place? What if *Leave It to Beaver* had been set in downtown Manhattan, if *All in the Family* had taken place on an American compound in Iran, or *The Dick Van Dyke Show* have taken place in 2016?

What are the settings of your life? How would things have been different if you had lived in a different part of the country or in an entirely different country altogether? What might you have struggled with if you had been born in a different generation? Going forward, are you going to change the setting of your life? What impact is that going to make?

Plot

The plot is the order or sequence of events in a story. Would the plot of your favorite show be different if the characters were a different ethnicity or if the protagonist had a profound mental or physical limitation?

Similarly, would the plot of your life be different if you were born into a different religion or a different socioeconomic class or with much more, or much less, intellectual capacity? It's kind of crazy to stop and think how fragile our lives really are and how their entire trajectory can be altered by one or two factors. What are the next big events in your life? When will they happen, and what changes come from each of those events?

Characters

The characters are the people in the story. It doesn't matter who we are or what we do; those around us affect our lives more significantly than just about any of the other factors. It helps to pay close attention to the company we keep and our beliefs about the company we keep. To fully understand the impact of the characters, imagine a character swap between *Leave It to Beaver*'s June Cleaver and *Game of Thrones*' Daenerys Targaryen, and you'll understand the impact and importance of characters!

Who were the characters in your life? How would your life be different if you had (or had not) been raised by an alcoholic or an abusive parent? Would the experience of being raised by an alcoholic or abusive parent be different if you believed that your familial situation was abnormal and shameful and something to be hidden, or if you believed that it was normal and acceptable and you could freely discuss your experience without shame? How we view the characters in our lives makes almost as big a difference as who those characters are.

Who are the characters in the screenplay of your life? What roles do they play? How do you feel about those characters? Imagine if one central person in your life had not been there and the impact their absence would have on you, as well as all the other characters in your life.

Now for the million-dollar question: Are *you* the main character in your own life? Ouch.

It is not uncommon for us to keep ourselves in orbit around others and to define our role in relation to them. You know, *I'm a wife* (to my partner, who is primary), *a mom* (to my kids, who are primary), *a lawyer* (to my clients, who are primary); you get the gist.

Right now I don't care about your roles or who else is in your life; I care about you. This is your story. Not your partner's, not your children's, not your clients', but yours. They each have their own stories. Of course, your stories intersect, but until you are clear on the role you play in your own (*spoiler alert* — you are the lead!), your character is probably not defined enough. Re-choreograph your life and make your third season all about you.

Theme

The theme is the philosophy, moral lesson, or central idea. Themes get tricky because most of our lives contain a series of intertwining ones, whereas in the entertainment industry the number of themes typically must be limited in order to produce a coherent show. For example, the theme of "family love conquers all" was portrayed week after week in *Family Ties* as the liberal ex-hippie parents and their conservative children were forced to reconcile their differences time and time again, but there were subplots and auxiliary themes that were played out between the various characters as well. In real life, many of our themes are not that coherent, consistent, or easy to spot.

What are some of the themes in your life? Are there themes that keep popping up again and again? I covered myself during late adolescence, while practicing law, and in navigating motherhood. Covering and subsequently losing myself was a theme that popped up several times for me, making it extra important for me to address if I wanted to grow. Take special notice of the themes that repeat in your own life.

Pretend you are in line at the pearly gates, chatting with the souls around you about the lives you just left. Was there an overarching theme to your life? Did the theme change as you grew, or did it remain consistent throughout your lifetime? How do you feel about this theme? Do you like it, or would you like to write a different one? The good news is, you are currently *not* standing in line at the pearly gates. You are here on Earth, and no matter how old you are, you still have time to make changes! What is your new theme?

Style

Comedy, sit-com, tragedy, soap opera, drama, romance, erotica, suspense, melodrama — there are many different styles that movies, television shows, or our own lives can take. Sometimes shows that are set in a different era, like *Mad Men* or *The Jetsons*, are given an exaggerated vintage or futuristic style. What if they had a different style altogether and had been produced as documentaries?

Just like our clothing, hair, and makeup, our — dare I say? — *lifestyle* is a reflection of our personality, our desires, the way we want to feel, and the way we interact in the world. Have you ever noticed that you have more energy and feel better about yourself on days that you look better? We don't have to be dressed to the nines or rocking leopard-print stilettos in order to feel good about ourselves, but the style we put forth into the world influences what we get back from others. If we look strong and confident, others treat us as strong and confident. If we look like day three of the stomach flu, others treat us like we are on day three of the stomach flu.

What is the style of your life? Is it extravagant or simple, messy or streamlined? Are you a harried single mom or a busy but centered single mom? Oftentimes we can change the entire tone and feel of our lives by simply being aware of the style we embody and changing it up. I am not joking when I say that how we *think* about ourselves affects how we *feel* about ourselves. If you can identify both the style of your current life and the style of the life you wish to attain, you can unequivocally *have* the life you wish to attain if you live and embody that style.

I'm not saying that you will go from being homeless to living in a mansion simply by changing your style. But I'm not saying that you won't, either! I'm simply saying that if your kids, dog, or partner or you yourself were up all night with the stomach flu and you feel like you were hit by a truck, you can make yourself feel better by shifting your style.

Let's say that the morning after the stomach-flu incident you have to drive car pool and lead a telephone conference at work. Can you feel the difference in your energy, outlook, and mindset if you:

(a) forgo a shower, put on your winter coat over your sweats, slap on dark sunglasses, and move through the day without brushing your teeth; or

(b) brush your teeth, take a quick shower, put on a semicoordinated yoga/fitness-like outfit, slap on some lip gloss, and pop in a pair of fun earrings?

I am not joking when I say that lip gloss makes me run farther and faster. It does. Style matters. Even when nobody sees you, style matters because it informs you about yourself.

Going back to your life and the style of your world: Does it have a slick, urban feel or a down-home, country one? Is your life a fairy tale, a rom-com, or a docudrama? Has the style of your life been consistent throughout, or has it changed? Are you currently experiencing a cohesively styled life; or does the style of your life differ between work and home depending on the people you are with?

I'm not talking about being more lighthearted with your

group of college friends than you are with your colleagues at the Society of Funerary Accountants. I'm talking about multiple-personality type of differences within your everyday world and relationships. Moving seamlessly in and out of a variety of different styles is healthy and enlivening. Living in a state of constant agitation, where you are constantly flipping into and out of a variety of identities, is not.

Is there anything you can do to re-choreograph your life that will create a more healthily consistent style to it? Remember your identity and brand, and find something concrete that represents your life's style.

This exercise is designed to give you a deeper understanding of your life as a story and of yourself as a character who is adept at playing a wide variety of roles. Perhaps these roles and scripts have fit you well, and perhaps they haven't.

Recognize and release what you no longer wish to carry. Going forward you have a choice. You can write your own script, or you can have somebody else write it for you. Nobody says you have to create your own life at all. You can create your own roles and play them how you feel they ought to be played, or you can accept the roles others give you. What will you choose, and what will you reveal?

Whip out that journal. Spend some thoughtful, quality time writing out the screenplay for season 3 of your life. You can be as detailed as you wish, or you can be rather vague, as long as you commit to following your heart. In my case, I had no idea that being a burlesque dancer was even a thing! There was no way I would have written a script for that, because I didn't know it existed. My script was about my commitment to the five steps of *FLAUNT!* My commitment was to follow my own rules, write my own scripts, and honor what my heart told me was right for me.

I found my fetish, laughed out loud, accepted uncondi-tionally, navigated the negative, and learned to let go fully, get naked, and trust in my truth. Through my commit-ment to *FLAUNT!* I found my Naked Self-Worth, and I re-choreographed a life that was far beyond my wildest dreams. Being a smart, spiritual, *and* sexy burlesque star was the result, and it was far better than anything I could have imagined.

I did the work. I recognized and released. Then I took a deep breath, stepped back, and let the Universe step in and work its magic. When my sparkly new destination appeared on the horizon, it was my turn to take up the reins and re-choreograph my life.

To build my dreams and live my sparkle.

Are you ready to build yours?

· · · · · • • ● ● ● ● ● • • · · ·

The Curtain Call

It's not the things we do in life that
we regret on our death bed; it is the things we do not.

— RANDY PAUSCH

*F*lip back and reread Shakespeare's "All the world's a stage"
intro to Act I. Can you see how all of us are merely players, playing our many parts over several ages? Shakespeare was
pretty darned insightful on that one, wasn't he? No wonder
we're still studying his works! You are a player in the story of
your life, and it is up to you to play each role exactly *As You Like
It*. (*Giggle*, see what I did there?)

Find your inner burlesque star, connect with your heart,
embrace every version of you that you have ever been, trust in
your truth, and reveal your core essence for all the world to see.
After all, you are the artistic director of your own life, and you
have only one opportunity to write a script that suits you. You
have one opportunity to be the star of your own life.

Act I is the past. It is over. Accept the lessons, integrate the stories, recognize it for what it was, and release what no longer serves you.

Act II is the present. It is here now. Reveal yourself in the ever-changing, ever-present moment. Stay awake, take center stage, and choose love. Find your fetish. Laugh out loud. Accept unconditionally. And when you do, you begin to write your future.

Act III is the future. As you re-choreograph your future and choose the path that determines what the rest of your life will be like, always remember to navigate the negative and trust in your truth.

The play is over. The curtain has come down, and the audience is on their feet cheering. It's time for the curtain call, where all the actors come out onstage and receive adulation and admiration from the audience. This was the play of your life. What story did you create? Were you the lead, the star of your own life? Did you act like it or not? How did you do? Are you satisfied with what you created?

What is your legacy? There's no room for regret or for politely waiting in the wings, hoping someone will turn the spotlight on you. They won't. Step into your own spotlight and take the leading role in your own best scenes.

When life is not going as you'd like it to, you have the ability to begin again, to rewrite and re-choreograph your life exactly as you see fit. This is your life. Not your kids'. Not your partner's. Not your parents' or your friends' or your employer's. It's yours. Wear what you want to wear, spread glitter all around, laugh at the irony, poke fun at yourself, play with the audience, and remember the titillating power of the tease! But above all, strip down and proudly reveal all that you are!

So you can be seen.
And known.
And accepted.
And loved.
For *you*.

All women deserve to be seen for who they are, not for what they do. All women deserve to feel the freedom and joy of standing in their Naked Self-Worth and knowing that who they are is more than enough. I believe that the five steps of *FLAUNT!* will get them there.

Find Your Fetish.
Laugh Out Loud.
Accept Unconditionally.
Navigate the Negative.
Trust Your Truth.
And don't forget to *FLAUNT!*

Acknowledgments

*I*t has been said that writing a book is a lot like birthing a baby. I wholeheartedly agree! In both instances I experienced weight gain, irrational bouts of crying, sudden and intense cravings, housework that I couldn't keep up with, a restructuring of my relationships and lifestyle, sleepless nights, fatigue, crippling self-doubt, fear, and ultimately unquenchable joy.

For about ten years I wrote down ideas, stories, and client experiences with the dream of incorporating them all into a book. But then I'd get scared. Scared of putting so much out there for all the world to see, scared of being wrong, judged, or not accepted for who I was and what I did. The irony is not lost on me. Finally, it became obvious to me that either I could sit on this 99.999999 percent complete book forever or I could drop my own cover and step into my Naked Self-Worth. And I'm eternally grateful that I did!

I'd like to thank the pole, dance, and burlesque communities for allowing me the grace, space, and acceptance to put my art onstage and move all that was inside of me out into the world and, in the process, set my soul free.

To my husband, family, and friends, for their undying support and love throughout my crazy journey. Thank you for not thinking I was an absolute lunatic for walking away from a really safe, secure corporate job that surely would have paid off my student loans and provided a nice, cushy retirement. Thank you for supporting me in becoming the wife and mom I wanted to be. Creating my own vision of a female-empowerment coach and becoming the world's first Life Choreographer has meant the world to me.

To my boys, Connor and Cody, you are the kindest, most honest and amazing human beings I have ever had the privilege of knowing. Your sense of self and your capacity for introspection are phenomenal. I admire your brilliance and your ability to make connections between and among things like nature, music, math, history, science, art, and literature. You are the most cultured individuals I have ever met, and without question, you will change our world for the better.

To my parents, for raising me to think that I could pretty much do anything I wanted, very rarely telling me no and instead showing me endless creative opportunities. And later, for perpetually watching my children, animals, or house (most of the time better than I would have) as I spread sparkle all over the world. Thank you for moving into the neighborhood and setting me free to be me.

To my husband, thank you for reading and editing endless drafts, for always saying yes to whatever direction I wanted to twirl off into, and for being at the ready every time I rang my "Press for Champagne" bell. Thank you for having the courage and strength to love me. I know it has not been easy.

To my friends, for allowing me to relegate our respective relationships to very bizarre terms where I was alternately *all in* and ready to play or completely incommunicado. Thank you for sticking by my side no matter what and believing in my crazy dream.

To my agent, Steve Harris, who instantly *got* me, saw my vision, and was able to offer insight that enhanced and clarified my work. Thank you for your direction and for your ability to state clearly and succinctly what I could do to make my proposal better, while at the same time telling me that I did not need to compromise anything I felt passionate about. Your guidance and patience in waiting as I stepped back and rechoreographed pieces of my work were invaluable.

To my editor, Georgia Hughes, wow, how I have enjoyed you and your wisdom! You were always spot-on with your thoughts, ideas, and comments about where to trim, where to expand, and what to clarify. Because of you, my book, from the cover to the content, is truly the embodiment of all I dreamed it could be. As a first-time author, who I am certain made her share of newbie mistakes, I never felt anything but warmth, encouragement, and trust from you. You are lighthearted and funny yet abundantly clear and sublimely brilliant all at the same time. You are my heroine in more ways than one.

I simply cannot say enough about Tristy Taylor, Kim Corbin, Kristen Cashman, Tracy Cunningham, Monique Muhlenkamp, Munro Magruder, Alexandra Freemon, and the rest of the team at New World Library. I am in awe of everyone I have had the pleasure of meeting or working with. Each of you has a glorious passion for books, a willingness to share the fun things that light you up as individuals, and the ability to create genuine connection in conversation. Every step of this process has been a dream, thanks to your expertise. I adore my book cover beyond measure, and the energy and joy I receive from you all — especially when you wear feather boas in sales meetings — is an absolute treat!

Index

About the Author

*F*ormer attorney turned female-empowerment coach, speaker, and radio personality Lora Cheadle encourages women to reveal their smart, sexy, and spiritual selves so they can fall back in love with who they are and find the satisfaction and fulfillment they crave.

Integrating her unique identities as an attorney, hypnotherapist, and aficionado of all things dance and fitness related, Lora works with women worldwide to identify and reveal the lost, covered-up pieces of their personalities so they can reveal and accept themselves as they are, not as they think they should be.

As a Life Choreographer, Lora is the creator of *FLAUNT!* and *Find Your Sparkle* coaching programs, workshops, and destination retreats, which utilize the concepts found in burlesque to show women how to playfully release self-judgment and integrate their beauty, brains, and beliefs into everything they do. She is the founder of the *FLAUNT!* Follies, a dance

troupe for women of all ages and abilities, and the *FLAUNT! Flock* Facebook group.

Named an Exceptional Woman of Excellence by the Women Economic Forum in India in 2019, she is beloved for her ability to provide practical tools that enable people to become happy, healthy, and free from burnout. She has written for *Elephant Journal*, coauthored a book in law school, and has a top-rated radio show, *FLAUNT! Build Your Dreams, Live Your Sparkle.* As her burlesque alter ego, Chakra Tease, she teaches and performs all over the United States, including Las Vegas, New Orleans, Los Angeles, and Hawaii.

A lover of the outdoors, she lives in Colorado with her husband and has two amazing sons. To learn more about Lora and her female-empowerment speaking and coaching programs, visit her website at loracheadle.com, or find her across all social media.